The Shells

That shaped my life

Farikanayi

ISBN 13: 978-0957627314 (Caroline Manyika)

DEDICATION

I wish to dedicate this book to those people who have faced extreme difficulties and survived; people whose spirit has sustained them (Proverbs 18:14) in the onslaught of physical, sexual, emotional, and financial or any other form of abuse and neglect. These are wounded people who refused and still refuse to bow down to the evil that sought to destroy them, showing that they are better than the bullies who assailed them and tried to harm them and mar their future. I thank them for refusing to become victims, for fighting back not the same way they were attacked but through turning their own lives around and kicking the past to the curb. May God commence, continue and complete the healing you need and for your pain may he recompense to you a double portion of peace, blessing, goodness, love and more peace. Don't give up now, let the sun of righteousness rise over you with healing in its wings (Malachi 4:2).

Table of Contents

ACKNOWLEDGEMENTS

Many things have happened leading to the point where a few years ago I decided to write this book. I started but it was a painful process so I more or less archived it. Between then and now I spoke to a couple of friends who had tough childhoods and have dealt with issues no child should even know about. Yet they are strong and they are here dealing with life one day at a time looking forward to a bright future.

Much has happened in the interim. I have listened to the word of God in and out of church. I have read the word for myself and found phenomenal scriptures that have changed my life. As I write now I am in a good place, I am in a place where my tears, those shed late at night when I was alone, have become a trickle rather than an avalanche. So who do I credit with my ability to now sit and write this book?

The vessels through whom the healing word has emanated aimed straight at a hurting heart and a troubled mind. I am privileged to sit at the feet of Wordpreaching, Word-teaching men and women of God who have been used by God as conduits for my healing. Because of the Word they teach, I can now write.

My babies: The children God decided to give to an insecure with low self-esteem and a fearful heart. He chose to use these lovely human beings to teach me love, loyalty, determination, persistence and perseverance and above all to bring healing to one who did not think she could ever be a mother. Because of their love I can now write.

I also acknowledge the role of the people who caused hurt and pain. They were selfish and abusive but they did not realise that God would still make an author of me even if it was through discussing what they did but which he turned round for my good. They didn't win. I did. So I can also say because of what they did, which God delivered me from, I can now write.

Intro

This has not been an easy project to embark on, yet it is a necessary one, not only for my healing but hopefully for that of whoever may still be hurting, emerging from whatever broken shells their life was encased in. What I will discuss, what I will explore and what I will re-live are very personal experiences which have mostly quietly shaped my life sometimes veering it so much towards despair that it is a miracle I am here and I am writing this without too much fanfare.

Of late I have become increasingly introspective and I have refused to continue to lie to myself about the state of my life, my upbringing, my past and the many scenes and acts I have lived through. I have realised that just because I have buried an episode of my life in my subconscious does not mean that it will remain there nor does it mean that I won't be aware of it. Unfortunately said episodes usually make their presence felt at very odd, awkward and usually inappropriate times. So I have decided to pre-empt their sometimes undesirable appearances by facing them and purposefully digging them up, exposing them and then giving them the boot.

What I have just said reminds me of an issue that plagued my family for years mainly before or around the time I was born. A few members of my dad's family suffered from epileptic fits. The incidents particularly with my dad were frequent and severe. One of the things I was told was that usually they occurred when there were crowds, or near a fire or river. My dad was a head teacher, and many of the times he had epileptic fits he was in front of students in the middle of assembly. He also has terrible burn scars on his legs and feet where he fell into but was thankfully pulled out of a fire before more of him was badly burned. It appears episodes occurred in places where the most embarrassment was caused or where the most damage could happen to him more severely.

It would appear some of the products of the shells I have emerged from have had similar aims and intentions. Looking at my life and that of people I know who have had similar issues to contend with, I can identify embarrassing or similarly destructive incidents whose aim has also been to wreak as much havoc as possible. It does not seem to be just about the 'incident' it also seems to be about the on-going almost perpetual impact of it. What I mean is that if you have gone through some destructive childhood experience, the destruction if uncurbed does not end with the initial occurrence but can become a lifestyle, or a lifetime occurrence or pattern.

Although I now love myself and appreciate who I am, it has taken a long time, effort and divine intervention to get me to this place. I have always found myself to be an enigma even to myself. I have done things and not really understood why I did them. I have made decisions I couldn't justify considering that I am actually an intelligent woman who can weigh up options and one would think that this would lead to sound choices but it hasn't always done so. And you needn't doubt my intelligence either because you don't get three degrees and a couple of professional certificates if your IQ is single digit. So it's not about how intelligent I am, because that is a given. Despite being intelligent, I have made some serious mistakes and I have had to work out why my life has been what it has been.

Because I have decided to face my life head on, I am now cutting the tentacles that have continued to extend their reach over the years and to clutch and pull me back at various stages in my life. I have decided to open the books I have kept in the library of my memory, unopened and gathering dust. I now want to know what I have not wanted to know, I want to once and for all challenge the issues that have been challenging my life and unceremoniously put them to a restless rest where they can't affect me but where they are also exposed and can't slither into other lives.

Another reason why I have decided to open these archived books is because of late I have realised that there are patterns in people's lives, actions some of the people I love have taken, decisions they also have made which have made me see the events of my life mirrored in theirs because like me they have unopened, unread, dust-gathering books in their subconscious which though closed, though archived have affected their lives just like they have affected mine. They now need to be opened, privately or publicly, and the contents now need to be read.

I know there are people who can put psychiatric, medical, theoretical, social and other definitions and explanations for what I am writing down. I am not trying to make an academic exploration of these shells because I prefer to write what I feel contested or otherwise rather than what paradigm claims to hold true.

What I will now explore are personal experiences and also observed patterns in the lives of people around me. I hope my power of observation is sharp enough to prevent me from making generalisations or assumptions. I pray also that what this book contains may save you or someone you love from years of unnecessary heartache and pain as you learn some lessons I have had to find out for myself, mainly out of desperation for a healing that is lasting and genuine. At the same time, I just need to reassure someone that the pain will ebb, dim, numb down then pass. I am a living testament of that fact. Refuse to have the past dictate your future, healing will come, but you need to extend your arms to it, you need to be ready for healing, you need to ask for healing and you need to be determined to be healed.

Death became life

(©farikanayi 7th May 2012)

Adversity had set a trap
I wasn't supposed to make it to this day
Hardship had sharpened its fangs for annihilation
What was meant for my harm became my blessing

Despair had rented a room
Claiming occupancy intending to stay
Fear taking up tormenting irrational residence
But all things have worked together for my good

Foolishness inaugurated
Reigning in financial relational choices
Lack had summoned her strong army to obliterate
But the arm of the Lord proved long enough to save

Self-doubt had a voice
Teaming up with inferiority and my past
Shame brought her shroud to cover my face to blind
But I am truly the righteousness of my God in Christ

Intimidation reigned
Highlighting failure promoting inability
Bedfellows with despising looks and marginalisation
But I can do all things through Christ as my strength

Life was ignorant
Of the pruning effect of the tough times
That even as I fell I looked up starting to rise again
Confessing that I am indeed more than a conqueror

Today I truly celebrate
What only Jehovah the Faithful can do
Bringing broken pieces together to unite in shalom
I am here aren't I the marvellous doing of the Lord

Chapter 1
The two shells

Because of the time and place I was born, my life emerged and was hatched from the shell of colonialism. This is a fact of my early life I had no control over. My parents may have had the opportunity to make a decision and their decision was to have a child. They received me, the product of a choice in times when choices and the ability to decide were rare and rationed. So I emerged at a difficult time when lives were contained in shells dictated by others, where parameters were demarcated by others and here I am.

Even as I emerged from the shell of colonialism, surrounded by its harsh realities, the erosions evident in bowed heads, the ridicule of grown men dressed in pressed shorts saluting those they should admonish, I was not to know I was in the process of being hatched from yet another shell. I must have been five or six years old when my life was linked to two people who rejoiced at my presence in their home and decided to use me for their selfish gratification. I emerged but was also contained in the shell of double sexual abuse by close maternal relatives. I was entrusted to them and they found me fair game for their selfish games.

Having said this, I really do need to find a quiet spot and read the books that chronicle these two shells. Both were authored in cruelty, both were authored in imposed rights of one taking from another what did not belong to them. Both shells that I have emerged from are just as dark, just as evil and just as destructive. And both have an impact that if not checked surpasses the years one was allocated to in this life into next generations and those beyond.

I didn't realise just how far reaching the effects of this double chord would have on my life. I didn't realise that it was affecting my life till I had to put this car into 'park', sit down and really ask myself some tough questions. I would have preferred to have got to this point sooner in my life but I didn't so I won't dwell on that. Maybe the fact that I have now got here and am now discussing this will help others whose lives are also spiralling out of control. Maybe the fact that I have stopped will make them stop at whatever age they are, at whatever point they have reached in their lives and they will also begin what I have begun, an honest introspective evaluation of their lives, a refusal to continue to walk down a road of pain, anger, bitterness, victim mentality, self-doubt, self-pity, unnecessary mistakes and shame.

I have to clarify something at this point, before I go any further with this exploration. This book is not about revisiting colonialism. Neither is it written from a victim mentality. It is not about racial issues nor is it about rehashing the past. One of the reasons why I have felt pressed to write it is because as I have seen the life patterns of others who have shared and emerged from common ground with me, I have realised that even though colonialism may be over, even though the abuse may have stopped, to those who experienced it, it may still be lodging in their homes and evidence of it can be seen in their attitudes towards people, in their decisions, in their failure to thrive in certain situations and sometimes in a fragility that does not match up with who they are or who they should be.

So this is not an opportunity to vent, been there, done that. Nor is it an opportunity to garner sympathy and commiseration. Another been there done that, don't need it. I don't write this from a point of weakness, when

I was at that point I couldn't have written it down, or if I had it wouldn't have helped anyone and I would have flooded my keyboard with tears, but I write dry-eyed cutting loose the hurt and pain and acknowledging that I have indeed come up, way up from the mud and mire and the slimy pit I dwelt in for so long (Psalms 40:2) after escaping from these two nasty old shells.

Something else I should mention at this point just to add clarity is the fact that people have emerged from different shells. Some people have emerged from shells of poverty. Even though they may now be in a better place financially, they still have certain ways of behaving that seem to be dictated by their past, by the pain of lack by the recollection of empty stomachs growling in the middle of the night robbing them of sleep. They may no longer be poor but they have not dealt with the poverty mentality that makes them horde things and that makes it difficult for them to buy the best within their means because they always have the nagging fear that they may return to the empty-belly times. So their financial decisions are affected by the shell of poverty, their relationships are affected and they either overcompensate for their times of lack or else they are such misers it hurts them to open their purse strings. Either way, the shell still has some level of power over them and they need to face it and deal with it.

For some people the shell that their story begins from is the shell of divorce. Their parents got divorced or they got divorced. They have quietly accepted divorce but have also quietly suffered from its lingering stigma, from unanswered questions about why it happened, from self-doubt, anger, rejection, fear and a host of other negative feelings for which they have not found a cure. As a result, they have buried the chronicles of the divorce hoping that in doing so they can get on with their lives. But these unresolved issues don't go away. They don't disappear like atrophied muscles which diminish from not being used. The unexplained tears still appear. The unexpected fear still shows up. The bad decisions and wrong choices are still made. The eruptive anger still occurs. They too need to visit the library of their subconscious on their own or with someone they trust and deal with these issues. They owe it to themselves, to their loved ones and to the people they relate with.

Maybe death, the death of a parent, child or close friend may be the shell that still sends its rays of despair through your life. When my cousin passed away a couple of years ago it took me a long time to accept that she was gone. She was my sister, my friend, my mother and my confidant. She was a safe place for me, somewhere I could be myself and somewhere my children were loved unconditionally. When she became ill I was angry with her. I didn't understand how she could be ill. It made no sense. She had been one of the strongest people I knew and she had previously defied death as she recovered from major surgery and as she recovered from other serious health challenges. So in my heart I was angry with her for succumbing to cancer as if it was her fault she had it.

I didn't understand my reaction to her illness. It made no sense. But the pain and confusion I now believe was linked to the fact that for most of my life I had not had a person or a place that I felt accepted me flaws and all and loved me without ever making me feel condemned. She actually was part of my healing process, because of her I had started to see what the past was doing to me, and now she was going!

I don't know how people deal with death, each person grieves differently and I am sure those who know best will tell us that there are stages we all go through when dealing with it. Maybe there are common stages, or maybe there aren't. All I know is that we all handle it differently and my reaction had a selfish slant to it in that although I was hurting for her, I was also hurting for myself by looking at what I was now losing.

There are some people that have opted for suicide because of the actions of bullies at school. How sad and painful it is for a life to end because another decided to persecute and torture them to the point where they felt there was no way out. How sad that maybe there was no one to understand what they were going through and encourage them to hold on and to face the issue in a different way, whatever that could be for them. The painful end of the matter is that the bully continues to live while they are dead and their family and friends have to deal not only with the loss of a loved one but also with the stigma of suicide and the self-questioning around it.

Just like I didn't choose to be born and raised during colonial times, or ask my maternal relatives to abuse me, most people have also emerged from shells of issues that were way bigger than themselves. It's only as their lives unravel and as their lives unfold that one notices some paradoxes and some oxymoronic behaviour which does not make much sense.

I remember a comment my dad made to me in sheer exasperation. He couldn't make sense of some things I had allowed to happen at a particular period of my life. This is a time that should have been the happiest of my life but it actually turned out to be a time of hurt, pain, disappointment and near despair which even led me to suicidal thoughts. My dad just couldn't understand how timid I seemed to have become, how wimpish. He said that he hadn't raised me to be a fool and a doormat and that he didn't understand what was happening to me.

What my dad didn't know was that I also didn't know what was happening to me. I was also as puzzled as he was. Later on of course when I was out of the situation the glances back brought shame and more self-doubt and timidity as I tried in my own way to escape things I didn't understand. I knew there was something wrong but had no clue as to its source or the fact that in my case I was trying to deal with a double portion of trouble from my past. Both shells were relentless in their attempt to destroy and cripple and unfortunately as I look around the people I connect with in life, sometimes I can see the cycles I have now escaped being repeated in some of their lives, I can see the results of the shells which may have fragmented and been destroyed just like colonialism has, or which may have been laid to rest as in the case of abusers who may now be old or dead. But the impact of them is still visible and still evident in lives still reeling, still trying to settle and still searching for both comfort and healing.

There are always symptoms that show or at least hint at lives that are being controlled by issues from the past, by incidents that have been buried deep but which still send their stench to the surface causing pain, disillusionment, wrong and really bad choices and sometimes disproportionate anger. Some of these will be common to particular causes but human difference may also raise some pretty peculiar symptoms.

Allow me to explore these shells and their impacts, not from a medical or psychiatric or psychological or even sociological perspective, but simply from a personal view, from what I have felt and experienced and also from what I see and have observed in the world around me.

Chapter 2
Some symptoms

One might ask why I am talking about colonialism now when it ended more than a decade ago in the nations where it lingered. And that of course is a good question deserving thoughtful consideration and needing to be answered. The reason is quite simple really. There are people, and I happen to be one of them, who lived during colonial times and are still alive. Colonialism then is part of their past, just like the first and second world wars are part of some people's past and just like the current wars in the Middle East are part of some people's past and present. There are people who lived during colonial times and they still carry the scars of those horrible times just like there are people whose lives were affected by the various wars different nations have been engaged in. Some still bear the wounds. They still need healing just like someone who has emerged from a shell of domestic abuse or civil war or anything else which causes physical, emotional, financial or psychological wounds. So to answer the question, as long as there are people who lived through colonial times and are still walking wounded, there is need to assess what happened to them and help them get help before the thing that is supposed to be in the past damages their present and their future. One of the nastiest aspects of colonialism just like any other forms of discriminatory politics was the stratification of society which eroded worth in some people and which dehumanised them in various ways. I am going to make a statement based purely on my own observations.

One of the symptoms of survivors of the shell of colonialism is denial of responsibility, or one could say shirking of responsibility. I have noticed it mainly in men. For years decisions were made for them. In a way they were feminised. They were relegated to kitchens and gardens and to menial tasks. Where before they were hunters and providers with clear demarcations of tasks and responsibilities, they were now delegated to the very kitchens they would never have been found in. They became cooks, and garden boys. They became people who took orders from kids they would normally have been disciplining not because they were ignorant or without intelligence but because of the melanin levels in their skin. As a result, many still dwell in those time zones where they expect their wives, girlfriends, mothers and everyone else to work and support them. They are totally confused about who they are, they have a huge chip on their shoulders but they are not willing to take responsibility and become leaders and heads in their families except by giving orders and barking at everyone the way they used to be barked at. They become replicas of the dictators they have loathed and despised.

Without some serious decontamination and some form of spiritual and emotional debriefing, the men who are like the ones I just described are a real paradox to their families. They want to give orders but they don't want to work and be the providers for their families. They expect the women in their lives to bow before them and to be timid and submissive then go and work for 12 hours a day to support them then come home and cook, clean and make love. They claim strength which is sometimes demonstrated through physical abuse but they can't or won't work. They are used to other people calling the shots and now that those who oppressed them are no longer there, they don't know what to do. They become a paradox. They blame everybody when things don't work out but they are not prepared to proactively do anything to change the status quo. They seem to turn their pain and transfer how they were treated onto their families. They have yet to be healed of the lingering battles emanating from their colonial shell.

Some of the survivors of colonialism can't make decisions; they never had the opportunity to do so, so whenever there are decisions to be made they have to consult 'friends' who advise them. They won't marry a particular type of woman because their friends don't approve, they won't make a financial decision until said friends have vetoed it. They were robbed of the ability to decide and so they still need 'friends' to help them decide. Some of them are perpetual 'mama's boys'. If mama says 'no' then that's it, the wife and children have to be under the all-powerful matriarch's control as well. These men's brand of intelligence was treated as if it was different from their masters' so they don't seem to be aware that they are now free and can revert to their own brain not their masters'.

This sounds harsh but talk to the women married to these men, talk to the children being raised by their wives while fathers lounge on the sofas and issue orders. Ask them why they are sitting at home with their academic and professional certificates gathering dust, unused in the labour market. Ask around, someone will explain how hard it is to live with a man who doesn't want to think but also oppresses those in his care and is intimidated when they start using their brains to change the situations they are in. The once oppressed become the new oppressors. And unfortunately, some of them fill church pews.

Let me state again that I am writing my own observations, I am not making any diagnosis, I can't because I am not medically or psychiatrically qualified to do so. All I can comment on is what I have experienced and what I have observed in the lives that have brushed shoulders with mine along life's journey. Not everyone reacts the same way even if they may be dealing with similar issues and escaping similar shells. I know many people who lived through colonial times and refused to allow the lingering effects to dominate their lives. They fought the system and have won over its on-going power. They know who they are in Christ and refuse to bow down in subservience and servitude except where it is right to give honour to another. So, not everyone who escaped colonialism is irresponsible or cruel, just like not everyone who was abused is abusive.

Not everyone that has been sexually abused continues to re-live the experience or to be bitter and angry. Some people seem to be more resilient, they seem to manage their emotions and their pain better than others. But many carry the pain and the scars and may erupt for no apparent reason. They may be timid or clingy, becoming obsessive when they do hook up with people. Trust remains an issue and as parents they can be obsessive about where their children are or about the people they allow into their children's lives. How do I know? Because I have walked down that road and it is not a pleasant place to be. Yet now as I read God's word I am told that he assigns my portion and my cup, God makes my lot secure and the boundary lines, the demarcation for everything that is me and that is mine, they have fallen in pleasant places and I have a delightful inheritance (Psalms 16:5-6). I no longer have sob stories; I now have a life-giving testimony.

From personal experience, I would say that one of the reasons why these shells are so destructive is because of the isolation they create and erect around the person who has experienced some form of abuse, especially so I think with sexual abuse. The shell requires secrecy because of the nature of what happens. So it isolates the abused person so that they have no support network. It bullies, bribes, humiliates and threatens them into silence.

My children love to watch nature documentaries where lions and other predators attack and kill zebra, buffalo and other animals. One of the things these animals always tend to do is isolate the targeted animal, once it is on its own it stands no chance. As long as your situation leads to your isolation, you lose out on the support network that could and should encourage and strengthen you. We were not created as islands. There is a reason why God puts us into families (Psalms 68:6) and communities, why he stresses and values good friendships (Proverbs 27:10; Proverbs 17:7; Proverbs 18:24).

My own experience was that I had no one I could talk to even if the childhood memories had surfaced earlier on in my life. I had no sister to confide in and no real friends to talk to. My mum was a disciplinarian before anything else and there is no way I could have even thought of talking to her about something like that. I think fear of her would have been greater than fear of what happened. Maybe that's why everything got buried so deep in my subconscious. Even though I was close to my dad even that wasn't the kind of relationship where I could go and say 'Eh dad, this is what so and so did during that time you left me at their house. Actually each time ... has been to our house this is what they have been doing to me...' Not a likely conversation in our household. Added to that, I was a very isolated girl, having no sister, being very shy and timid, I preferred my own company and spent a lot of time daydreaming. I was isolated and only had me to consult when dealing with difficult issues. My aunt, the person I could have shared stuff with because of the nature of our relationship was too busy being bitter and dealing with disappointments life had dealt her decades before, she was not and could not be a comfort to anyone. So I was isolated.

In secret then this stuff eroded my self-worth and though I may sometimes have appeared jocular and out-going the reality especially so to a child's mind was that the whole world was out to get me. So tears were a constant companion. Irrational, terrorising fear became a constant, crippling, unwanted bedfellow. Who could I tell? Unfortunately I was also teased mercilessly about being always scared, no one knew why and unfortunately no one tried to find out why so it continued. My parents didn't understand my fear; my brothers had a field day making fun of me for being scared of everything. I remember being called a cockroach because I was so timid and scared. I couldn't watch television because any kind of fighting had me covering my eyes, I couldn't stand any kind of violence and I seemed to always want to placate people if disagreements seemed likely so that there wouldn't be a fight.

Looking back I believe both the abuse and colonialism contributed to some of the symptoms that have dogged my life. Low self-esteem partnered sometimes with a massive chip on the shoulder and a knack for analysing people's words for hidden meanings. Both contributed to fear and also to low confidence and to a need to always prove myself even when there was no need to. Both made me overly protective of my children never wanting any of them to live my experiences. Both also made me overly aware of my flaws and both contributed to a despising of who I am, how I look, and the essence of who I am, who God made me. Both made it difficult sometimes to connect to God blaming him for not seeing and not helping me, creating me as ugly and undesirable.

I must have been such a contradiction and a true enigma to the people around me as I exhibited both strength and weakness concurrently, both joy and sadness and a crippling shyness that led to people assuming that I was aloof or standoffish. I didn't like mixing with white people always immediately putting myself on a lower societal rung and at the same time assuming that they were also putting me on the lower rung. What a process of healing I have needed and thankfully now got.

How easy then it is to get involved with wrong men or women when you have such low self-esteem. One just needs to compliment you on your dress, or attire and you are so anxious to feed on what else they have to say about you, so anxious, in fact desperate to be with them even if they rob you blind, as long as they can say some nice things about you, as long as for the two seconds they stay in your life they make you feel as if your body is actually beautiful and desirable. Relationships become an addiction. You are so desperate to be loved and to be accepted, to be found attractive that you become blind to who the person is, the user, the abuser, the cheater, the neglectful, the sarcastic and cruel person you are claiming to love and believing to be loved by. But unfortunately, you can't get affirmation of worth from a person; that's something only you can confer as you align your thinking about yourself with what God who created you has to say about you.

So you feel dirty after each relationship and move on until the craving for another shot of fake compliments kicks in and you get into another relationship and until the cycle is broken, this can become a life-time pattern leaving you worse and worse each time but without a way to stop. Unfortunately it can also leave you with unplanned responsibility as you may end up with children from each relationship. Even though God forgives, the children can become a constant reminder of your failure, of your weakness, of the mistakes you made. The children are not a mistake, they didn't ask to be born, and they remain a blessing from God. Their presence just reminds you of the pain from the relationship, of the poor judgement and the person you shouldn't have hooked up with in the first place. Your desperation for what you thought was love becomes the issue that perpetuates your pain and generates bitterness as relationships end and you despise yourself more and more.

Family and friends will of course judge you for your choices; they will condemn you and talk about you. Some will have a field day with your mistakes ping-ponging them around in their circles of discussion. Yet none will try to find out what it is that makes you behave as you do. You become an enigma, a mystery even to yourself and unless and until you find a way to break the cycle of bad and wrong choices, you could be set on the road to a very repetitious life of questionable choices, pain, regret, shame and back to the same choices, living in an explosive and cyclic pattern until something gives.

What I find really sad now is looking into the lives of some of the people I love and seeing them live the life I lived even as Christians, spinning in their own cycle of bad choices and regret, starting again with good intentions and going back again to the bad choice. I see the pattern of my life replicated in theirs and it hurts to know that they are hurting like I did but they don't know who to tell or how to get help. But the good news is that the word of

God is indeed sharper than any two-edged sword (Hebrews 4:12) and if we let it, will cut through the ribbons binding that vicious cycle in place. It will bring the healing we all need and it will direct us to the one who is our help (Psalms 121).

We know that with God nothing is impossible (Luke 1:37, Genesis 18:14) so even your situation is not impossible, your issues are not so hard that they cannot be solved, even your pain can be healed, even your shame can be wiped out and even your bitterness can be stemmed and stopped so that you become a person of confidence and soundness in all you do.

People react differently to the shells they emerge from. Some bear up better than others. Some stoically push forward with life, others crumble and appear delicate. But whether they appear tough or fragile, they still need help and support to acknowledge the source of the pain and to get the healing they need. If they don't seek and get help, incidents that occurred in their youth can mar their teens, adult life, middle age and even old age. The impact of the shells can be long and far-reaching but it can also be stunted and broken so that it no longer affects life.

Chapter 3
Some consequences

There is a sad truth regarding the choices we make and I can hold my hand up to the fact that what I am about to say is something I have observed in my life and in the lives of people around me who have emerged from different shells or maybe those similar to what God has rescued me from. His grace is sufficient for each of us (2 Corinthians 12:9) if we tap into it and I am so grateful for that because had it not been for his grace our actions would have killed many of us off years ago. I know I wouldn't be alive today if God hadn't rescued me from myself. I was on a self-destructing path and blaming the world and the planets for it. You see when you emerge from some of these shells you sometimes lose the will to live and you do things that would normally kill. But his grace is sufficient, I don't know why it is but it is and once again I can only say 'Thank you Lord'.

Looking at my life, I can only imagine that God really has a purpose for me. There has to be a reason why he has fought me to keep me alive. There has to be a reason why he hasn't allowed my choices to kill me or to permanently damage my life leaving me unable to carry on. I can't take this grace for granted; I can only be in awe of him and his goodness to me. I am thankful to be alive, I am thankful to now be in a situation where I can look back and not feel the gnawing pain that seems to have been a constant companion for me for many years.

The last four years or so have been crucial to my healing. I cannot pinpoint a specific time where I suddenly became healed. I believe it has been an accumulation of incidents, a layering of words, an aggregate of virtue dripping into my life through good friends, a good church, anointed men and women of God, a yielding to his word and his will, a desire to be healed, a determination to experience the best he has for me, an appreciation of his love and a host of other things all targeting my life, chipping away at the fear, dropping in confidence, correcting in love, covering my wounds with his healing balm, reassuring me of my worth and pointing out who I am in Christ.

I am grateful, I am thankful that where I am now is not where I was 4 years ago or even two years ago. I can see what has happened in my life, I can acknowledge the fading scars and the fact that the searing pain has ebbed then gone. I have much to be thankful for and as you read my confession and my testimony, I pray that you will be encouraged and that you will receive the same help I got and years sooner than I did and at a faster pace than I allowed myself to be healed. Take comfort in knowing that the past regardless of how vile it may have been, can be just that, past, gone, ineffective, powerless. Yet there is another truth that also emerges, the fact that you are alive means that your past did not kill you. In fact for all you know it may have made you a stronger person. How do I know this? Because that is how I feel about myself. I survived which means that I am strong, I am stronger than I would have been had I not gone through and come through to the other side. You can't measure your strength without something that tests it.

I read these words and they echo so much with me:

> 'There is only one thing that I dread: not to be worthy of my sufferings'
> (Viktor E. Frankl: 2004 Man's search for meaning. Rider London p75)

I'm sure there is a more academic meaning that can be derived from these words. But for me what I understand of them is that I have not had bad experiences for no reason. They were bad, they were horrible but something good has to emerge otherwise my pain would have been just that, pain and nothing remotely positive can be gleaned from it all. But I refuse to accept that. As a mother I have experienced excruciating pain when I gave birth to my children. But that was not wasted pain. My babies were the end result of it. So any pain I have suffered in other areas of my life will also yield something good even if the good thing is that I can tell my story and someone else gets healed or someone else becomes hopeful about their future. Or maybe the positive result is the fact that I can testify of God's goodness and I can say that the thing that was meant for my harm, to destroy my life has been turned round for my good (Genesis 50:20) and it has become a life giving force to another. I am stronger in my faith. I am stronger in my character. I am more forgiving because I too have been forgiven. I have learned some valuable lessons which I can pass on to someone else so that they don't have to remain where they are but can be healed and move on. So take these words on board, your suffering, your pain has not been in vain. Ensure that something good emerges from that shell. If you let it destroy your life then it has been in vain. If it leads another to healing, then something good has come out of it, take joy in that.

I just read the book of Ruth and at the end is a summary which according to the thoughts of man should not even be in the bible. We expect perfection of ourselves and each other sometimes and we fail to realise that God works with hearts not with qualifications (2 Chronicles 6:30; Jeremiah 17:10). Sometimes I think he just uses things we despise to show that he is God and to destroy our prejudices. Ruth 4:18-22 (like Matthew 1: 1-17) lists one of the most imperfect groups of people I have read about in the whole bible and yet they form an important link in the genealogy of our Lord. Look at this mixed bag of 'sainthood':

➢ Pharez: his mother was Tamar who dressed as a prostitute and went and slept with her father-in-law Judah when he wouldn't give her a husband (Genesis 38)

➢ Judah: about whom the bible says that the sceptre of righteousness shall not depart from between his feet (Genesis 49:10) but he along with his brothers tried to kill their younger brother Joseph, the same Judah who solicited the services of prostitutes

- ➤ Rahab and Salmon: Salmon married a prostitute who was well known and has continued to be referred to in the bible as Rahab the harlot (Joshua 6; James 2:25; Hebrews 11:31; Matthew 1:5)
- ➤ Ruth was a Moabitess, a foreigner, a widow, a despised person because of her country of origin. I can certainly identify with that having lived in both USA and the UK and knowing what it feels like to be a foreigner and to sometimes experience people's criticism not because of anything I have done but because of where I come from, because of being a foreigner (like Ruth)
- ➤ David who killed a man to get his wife (2 Samuel 11), yet became the yardstick against which Kings were measured (2 Kings 18:3)

None of these people deserved to be even mentioned in the bible let alone to be the ancestors of our Lord, if we were to follow the world's standards. Yet here they are.

In the book of Samuel a self-righteous woman called Peninnah tormented her rival Hannah because Hannah was barren (I Samuel 1). What she didn't realise was that even though Hannah was barren at this time that was no indication of Hannah's life in a year's time. She didn't know that it is God who opens wombs. Looking at your life you may feel as if it is a barren life, relationships aren't working, finances aren't working, and children are like yoyos you never know what to expect next. Stop and meditate on the beginning and the end of Hannah. God knows the beginning from the end of your life and each matter relating and pertaining to you (Isaiah 46:10). He wants to work with you so that you have the end he planned for you, he wants you to have the glorious end (Haggai 2:9) even if the beginning may have been riddled with pain, abuse, shame, anger, unworthiness and anything else you can add to this list.

Whatever happened in your life, whatever shells you have fought your way out of, keep in mind that this does not dictate the path your life follows, nor does it seal your future and your end. People say that children who are abused end up as abusers. But I know for a fact that there are many who were abused who have turned out to be upright citizens of their generation and wonderful parents to their children. Nothing is set in stone.

God says that he will perfect that which concerns you (Psalms 138:8). This tells me that there is hope as it also says in the word that to the living there is hope (Ecclesiastes 9:4). Therefore there is flexibility, there is room for change, and there is room also thank God for hope and for both optimism and faith. How you began is not and does not have to be how you end. A runner may start off in a crouching position; if he or she remains in that position we never get to know what a sprinter they are. They have to move from the crouch and take the first step then build up on that until they break records or run their race the best they can. You may feel like you are crouching, like there is no speed in you because the things that have happened to you have knocked the wind out of your sails. But take heart. Christ is both the author and the finisher of our faith (Hebrews 12:2). If you let him, he can and will make sure that he sees you to an amazing finish, he will be your shepherd, taking you through whatever stages of healing you need to pass through until you can relax and rest in the lush, green pastures he has for you (Psalms 23). Don't be fazed by your beginning, don't let it overwhelm you. His grace is sufficient for you (2 Corinthians 12:9) and he has some good stuff ready for you if you turn to him for help.

Hannah went to God; she didn't try to fight her tormentor. She knew that was a futile battle and so she went to the one who has the answers. She cried to him, he heard her, he opened her womb. He gave her children whose names are written in the bible. Mm.., I don't recall Peninnah's children's names, nor do I know what they did or what became of them. But I do know that Hannah's son Samuel became a mighty prophet, in fact my parents named my brother after him and I named my son after him.

But what happened to the tormentor? She faded into insignificance when God did what only he can do, he raised his daughter from insignificance and reproach and made a barren woman the mother not only of one son, but of 5 more children, three sons and two daughters (1 Samuel 2:21). If we let God, you and I are in for some promotion, for some womb opening, barrenness breaking, stature instilling blessing. He's done it before so I know he will do it for me and he will do it for you, just because he can and just because he loves us and he wants to bless us.

Sometimes the shells we emerge from are of our own making. We don't always want to acknowledge that we may be responsible for some of our own troubles. For example, Sarah introduced Hagar into her marriage (Genesis 16:1). Abraham received Hagar into his marriage (Genesis 16:14). We can spend all day debating who was right and who wasn't, or who should have known better and who should have said a resounding 'no'. But such are Abraham and Sarah's lives. They are littered with instances that leave us with questions rather than answers but they are also full of happenings we can identify with when we are being truthful and honest to and with ourselves. The reality is that Hagar was introduced into this marriage and pain and strife came with her. Sarah and Abraham were responsible for the trouble that came because of Hagar and he offspring.

Even in that we learn a valuable lesson. The point is not really who is to blame or who did want to whom. Life does not get better because you blame everyone in it. Your situations don't improve just because you were hurt or even that you can locate the origin of your pain. You just continue to hurt and you continue to make the wounds fester as long as you are at the point of blaming someone or something. You can't find healing while you are focussing on who did this or that thing to you. You have to get to the point where you acknowledge the hurt but deprive it of its potency by refusing to let it continue to torment you.

There is no debating whether or not God forgives us for the things that happen in our lives, the things we do or neglect to do. His son died so that we can have that forgiveness. Unfortunately even though we are forgiven, sometimes there are aspects of our actions that we cannot get rid of. Thankfully the Isaacs do come and the Hagars may eventually go away, but the Ishmaels may be there to haunt us, as a consequence of some of our less brilliant decisions and choices.

A child born out of wedlock is not an Ishmael, they haven't done anything wrong and they are a blessing from the Lord. But the consequences of having a child at that time may haunt you. Some men may judge you deciding not to marry you and raise 'someone else's child'. You may have to contend with the financial, social and emotional difficulties that plague single parents. There is the stigma in some places and the fact that there will always be someone who knows you intimately even though you wish they didn't. The virginity you lost can't be recouped. The stretch marks you now have give away your state of motherhood even before you say you have a child. You may have to contend with knowing looks from the 'holy' people in church and there are opportunities that may become difficult to access as you try to juggle child care, work and your own needs on a tight time and money budget.

Maybe it is divorce whose effects and tentacles still impact your life. Regardless of why the divorce happened, you still have to deal with the results of it, the consequences of it. The issue like the introduction of Hagar into the Abrahamic equation is not who was right and who was wrong in the marriage even though most divorcees have their hand stretched out and their finger permanently pointing at the other party stressing their mistakes. The issue is that the divorce happened, a marriage failed and there will be Ishmaels emanating from it who will hurt not just the two who made the decision to divorce but also their families and their children. There will be awkward moments when friends you had in common when you were married now have to choose who to relate with. And many will add to your pain as they choose sides or as they ostracise you because of the divorce. Many will make judgemental statements and many will act as if they know it all as they give useless advice. But these are Ishmaels you can't ignore even if you didn't initiate the divorce.

I know people I used to consider to be friends, people who were 'close' to me who have shunned me and taken sides without ever even speaking to me. The strength of their friendship was tested and found wanting. Then there are others who have stuck with me through thick and thin and have refused to leave me even when I was pushing them away. There are others who are like Reuben, having the character of water, freezing in the cold, melting in warm, evaporating when the heat is on. They are the friends you really don't need because they leave your back uncovered. So there will be consequences, loneliness as people desert you, pain as friends defect, hurt as words fly cross-country or even cross-continent. But regardless of all this, you still owe it to yourself to live and to be the best you can be. True friends will remain. Let the fakes and the judges go. You don't need them. God will give you new friends, genuine friends. I have people in my life now who don't seem to see behind me to my past or to the mistakes I made. They have God's eyes and see me as he sees me. Of course even now there are judges who try to ram my head with their gavel. But praise be to God I don't need them and I don't give them the time of day.

Losing your virginity as a result of abuse or rape can make you bitter against the people who did it to you. But one thing to acknowledge once you are able to sit and assess your life is that you can't change that fact but you can change your future by the way you regard the issue. You may have become sexually aware at an early age because of this person but that does not mean that you should then decide to become sexually active. The nose you end up spiting is your own not the other person's. Anything you do, regardless of the reason, becomes your responsibility. If you catch a sexually transmitted disease or if you get pregnant or if you abort a pregnancy, those are now choices you make. You may be behaving a particular way because of what happened to you which is setting you on a dark path, but you still have the power to choose what you do. Wrong choices will now become the Hagars that breed Ishmaels that wreak havoc in your life. A link in that chain has to be severed and the choice and responsibility once again falls on you.

What am I saying here? Bad things do happen and many may have happened to you. The power they have over you is the power you surrender to them. You can and must decide that the abuse, the divorce, the bad thing that happened is not granted access into your future. It cannot continue to hurt you and it will not impact your future. If you don't make this choice then you suffer double tragedy, the act in the past, its consequences in the future. So find a way to assess where you are, what you are feeling and make a conscious decision to boot the past back to where it came from. Deny it access into your future. Cut the thread of pain it has wrapped around you.

The following words emphasise the need to put things in perspective and move on:

> *You can either go by the pull of your past, or by the pull of your future. At every point in time, both*

your past and your future are speaking to you. Your past is calling you to what you have done (I will add here: or what has been done to you). Your future is calling you to what you can do. Your past is looking back at your lowest performance. Your future is looking forward to your highest potential. Your past is reminding you of your failures. Your future is reminding you of what can be done through the grace of God. You have to choose which voice you will follow, and which path you will take (Dr Mensah Otabil. Facebook comment 24th October 2012).

Reflect also on these words and let their meaning seep into your very being. It's one sentence which is packed with meaning:

I can be changed by what happens to me, but I refuse to be reduced by it (Maya Angelou).

There are some voices that are worth listening to when you need help. Voices that speak not only from what they have encountered and overcome but voices that have helped in others' healing process. Then of course there are some other voices that you shouldn't listen to because instead of healing they bring death, condemnation, judgement and an even greater sense of shame and self-recrimination. Here is an excerpt from a voice that has been crucial to my healing:

> *As God positions you for the future, you will begin noticing the importance of breaking old cycles. Breaking the cycle of repeated mistakes requires making a decision to move on with your life, but it won't happen overnight and neither will it be easy. Find a way to move out of the past, move ahead, free from all encumbrances that threaten to leave you attached to your yesterday. Do not let the dead weight of old cycles impede your progress! (TD Jakes WTAL - 52 Days of Pecking Orders - Day 18 Facebook post 25th October 2012)*

This last entry highlights some important things to consider:

- You have a future, if you are still alive that means there is probably a tomorrow for you to look forward to
- The past can be perpetuated in cycles, repeating patterns which include repeated mistakes and bad choices
- The cycle can be broken but you have an active role in that snapping of the chord tying it in place connecting it to your future
- Breaking the cycle is neither automatic nor instant, it needs time and it definitely needs effort
- There is a way to disconnect from the past and you need to make an investment into finding the way
- The past, a bad and painful past is cumbersome, and it threatens your future, it's aim is to remain in your now and in your tomorrow but it is not a positive presence and so you need to break away from it
- Lugging your past along hinders your future, it is a deadweight, it needs to be offloaded and buried
- You must move on

What should you do? Acknowledge your need for healing and your need for help. Allow God and good people access into your life and let him bring the healing you need. Find out how what happened back then is affecting you now. Take time for some honest reflection and introspection; put things in perspective and determine not to allow what happened in your past to mar, diminish, blur, taint, destroy or inhibit your bright future. There are decisions you can make which will bury your past and cause you to arise to a light you never thought could be yours but which has always been available to you (Isaiah 60). You couldn't see it through the blur of tears and through the shield of pain and hurt. But as you receive your healing, your sight, your vision will improve and sharpen. You will stop seeing people like trees (Mark 8:24) and begin to see things, life and situations the way God sees.

Chapter 4
Getting a diagnosis

It is really strange for something to be wrong with you but for you not to know it or not to know the extent of it. Now I am not a doctor, nor am I in any way medical, as a result, I put a disclaimer here that I don't know what makes people behave like they do, I don't know what may ail them. But one thing I do know is that there was certainly and definitely something wrong with me. I may not have known or understood the seriousness of it, but along the way I had to eventually acknowledge that there was something seriously wrong.

I have also in the last few years found a way to identify the problem areas. God gave me these things called tears which have become very good and accurate thermostats for me. I know I am a bit of a cry baby and that is a family trait which affects male and female members of my whole extended family. Tissue companies make money off us and when we have family gatherings it's quite comical to see the tears rolling down old and young, male and female, educated and uneducated cheeks alike. We probably cry just as much at weddings as we do at funerals. It's our inheritance. We cry. Maybe it's this familiarity with tears that has made me aware of how they work for me. There are times when something quite apparently random triggers the tears. I used to just cry and move on but now that I know that my tears have a purpose, and I am serious about this, I have started to see when they fall inexplicably. They have become a useful gauge of the presence of those tentacles from old shells.

I know sometimes people lie even to themselves. They seem quite determined to be actors in unpaid roles. They do all they can to convince not only the people around them but also themselves that they are fine and that there is nothing wrong. But there are times when truth takes charge, then the tears fall unchecked or anger erupts without justification or reasonable provocation. When there is no audience to perform for, when the stage is bare, all props dismantled and packed away the make-up has been removed and truth and honesty demand to be heard, then the tears, the self-loathing, self-recrimination, the shame and reality all converge refusing to hide behind the camouflage of a pasted smile, refusing to be denied access. A cycle emerges and can be repeated daily if the scissors of truth is not permitted to snap the ribbon of fakeness.

Whatever it is that causes the nightly weeping has to be addressed and dealt with. Whatever wounds bleed in the secrecy of the night need to be bound up and allowed to heal. Whatever secrets are buried so deep that guarding them becomes a full time preoccupation also need to be dealt with so that their potency is cut down then wiped out. One should sleep when it's time to sleep not be tormented daily by the past which continues to be allowed access albeit secretly into the present.

Another way people seem to deal with their pain is by magnifying the problem to the extent where it appears unique. It is easy to make yourself such a special case that you exclude yourself from possible healing because in your sight no one else has ever experienced what you have gone through and so no one else can possibly have the antidote or the cure for it. The bible says that there is no temptation any of us faces which is not common to all men (1 Corinthians 10:13). There is no issue any of us deals with which is entirely unique, Solomon tells us that there is nothing new under the sun (Ecclesiastes 1:9) and this applies to our pain. I believe that one way to deal with it and to begin to be healed is to cut your close ties with the issues that have assailed your life. Instead of talking about it in a personal and possessive way as if it belongs to you I believe that relinquishing that relationship helps. Make it a stranger to your heart, your time and your speech, deny it pride of place and starve it of the attention it has been thriving on as you have fed it and elevated it.

Once you know that what has happened to you has happened to others, it becomes easier to look at others and accept the healing they have also received. Your hope can be stirred up as you see people getting on with their lives and refusing to become victims of whatever circumstances and whatever shells may have shaped their past.

The diagnosis of the past does not need an expert. What it takes is an honest assessment of your own life. It takes a desire to change what is not working so that your life can be better than what it currently is. It takes refusing to have lonely pity-parties holding a nightly vigil over issues that should have been buried a long time ago but have instead been left to stink up your space each time you remove the cloak over them and rehash their history and revisit them.

Understanding an issue can be the beginning of its destruction. If you were abused, it's not your fault; it's the abuser's fault. They shouldn't have done it. Acknowledging and accepting this might help you understand some of the things you do. Although it cannot justify substance misuse or whatever way of coping you may have been using, at least it can point out why you do it so that you can deal with it.

It takes a lot of courage to dig up painful issues and sit through an analysis of them. It also takes a lot of courage to honestly evaluate your life on your own and to unemotionally separate the various aspects of it and admit that you have done some things wrong, that you have lacked wisdom, that you have been fearful or that you are bitter. Sometimes if you are blessed to have good people in your life they may tell you and this may be the wake-up call you need so that you evaluate your life and see what needs changing and what issues may need addressing. You may need to seek professional or spiritual help, do whatever it takes; your future depends on it.

This is a crucial part of moving forward. If you hold on to all the mess surrounding your life, it weighs you down. It's difficult to travel swiftly with baggage all over you. Even in a natural form of travelling, if you have no luggage you can walk faster and get further more quickly than someone with two or three heavy bags that they need to lug with them. If you are carrying bags of bitterness, hate, anger, fear, mistrust and whatever other nasty stuff has stuck to you as a result of abuse or whatever shells you have emerged from, you may also be holding yourself down slowing yourself down and hindering your progress to wherever you need to get to with your life. Baggage is heavy.

Find out what it is you are carrying, and offload. Don't be taken by surprise when you discover that you are bitter and angry and maybe you find this out when people always leave you. You are a good person but people don't hang around with you because they are fed up of your sarcasm and cutting comments, they are fed up of your prejudices or the nasty speech that always emanates from your mouth. So check and see what is wrong, and stop punishing people for what happened to you before they even knew you.

You can't get into a meaningful and healthy relationship with someone and bring in lodgers to share the relationship. Just because you get married does not mean that the fear or anger will go away. Just let your husband or wife do something wrong and every closet will fly open as your baggage comes to your rescue. Your spouse won't even know what has hit them! They begin to pay for every hurt you ever experienced. The person who loves you becomes your physical, emotional and verbal punch bag and chances are they will leave.

Be honest enough with yourself to acknowledge that you have become an angry person and that you lash out at people who are close to you and who try to love you. Admit it if you have been using people getting in and out of relationships to try and bridge the emptiness you feel inside, but each time you have had a relationship you quickly left it as you realised that it didn't cure the loneliness and the pain. So you moved on and tried again and again and again and now you are in a situation where you could be described as promiscuous, not because you are a bad person, just someone trying to find healing in the wrong places. No man can cure what is wrong within you. No boyfriend, no husband just like no girlfriend or wife can cure what ails you. You need to come to them whole otherwise you turn your relationship into a hospital when it is supposed to be a place of building a future.

Maybe you have been trying to find ways to just forget the painful past and drinking worked for a while but now it doesn't and you have to keep trying harder stuff, things that are causing damage to you socially, emotionally or even physically and financially but which seem for a while to numb the pain. But once you are sober the pain returns with vengeance so the cycle continues becoming even more vicious. Band-Aid solutions don't work for big wounds. Over the counter pain killers may not have sufficient strength to solve your problems. In fact until you get a diagnosis, any treatments you embark on will either be useless, experimental, hit and miss or even harmful. You have to match the cure to the disease.

Confront these issues, address them and do something about them. Don't allow them to continue to simmer awaiting explosion when least expected. Get a diagnosis of what is wrong and allow God to prescribe the best healing tonic for you. Healing is yours but you need to receive it. You need to acknowledge your need for it. Christ says something in Matthew 11:28 we can apply to this situation. He tells those who labour and are heavy laden to come to him and that he will give them rest. I can't think of a better way to diagnose and demonstrate the healing process. God knows that emerging from shells leaves us with loads, burdens and baggage. He knows how laborious it is to try and live while carrying guilt and fear, anger and bitterness. He extends his hands to us and tells us to come to him, to bring our issues and cast them at his feet (1 Peter 5:7), to him they are light but to us they are burdens and they hinder our movement and progress. But we have to come to him, we have to bring the load to him, we have to decide that it is too heavy and it is unnecessary baggage. We have a part to play.

What people don't always realise is the fact that just because the issue is buried, ignored or hidden does not mean that it is dead. Many times it festers, simmering quietly out of sight and sometimes out of range of our daily memory but a time comes when it erupts and if there is no sound help in place, it can destroy yet again a life already destroyed by another's actions.

I am putting my thoughts down in the hope that someone reading this will realise that hiding abuse will not make its results go away. Acting as if it never happened will not automatically destroy the impact of it. If you were abused, you need to deal with it, you need to be healed and you need to deal with the buds of hurt, pain and anything else shooting out as a result of it.

My hope then is that although it might hurt to recall, you will still actively seek and get help and allow the wound to be healed so that you can stem its invasion into your present and future. I pray that you will have the strength to deal with whatever aspects of your past have emanated from the abuse so that what happened to you does not have a domino effect hurting you and others again and again and again because you have hoped that you are well rather than knowing for a fact that you are well.

Let me conclude this part with the following quote:

Self-pity is the worst illness a man can contract. Saying you are a victim strips you of resourcefulness. Every seed for your future is in you (Dr Ramson Mumba FB post July 3 2012)

Chapter 5
Intermittent mini shells

Most people can probably identify what I will call the 'major shell' in their lives just like I have with sexual abuse and colonialism. These may be shells that have really left their lives fractured and the person disillusioned, hurt, in despair, angry, bitter and usually in blame-mode. These could be things like death, divorce, rejection, and a host of other shells whose impact lingers until they are dealt with and purposefully smashed to bits. Some people may be emerging from a conglomerate of major shells, maybe a combination of things that happened all at once, and they provided a corporate impact, they destroyed or hurt conjointly not singly. So maybe you feel as if there is no hope because of the intensity of your experiences.

But along life's journey, just like little aftershocks, each shell can cause little mini-shells to also form and crack. There is nothing mini about their impact. They are only mini in that they tend to be a result of a major shell, like an offshoot, or a bud on a given plant stem. Yet their impact can be just as crippling if they are left unchecked, untreated, unhealed.

It's a sad truth that trouble seems to love company. It tends to visit with its siblings, cousins or extended family and it comes packed for a long stay. Usually as you identify one mini-shell it is easy to also see another lurking behind it and another sidling up to impose its own brand of venom. I sometimes think that like the devil trouble comes set on inflicting the most possible damage, destruction and death which is why its attacks tend to be intense. A father dies and as his family is dealing with his death along comes debt clamouring for attention. As the family deals with financial loss they may lose their home and end up living with relatives who may not be too happy about this and may emotionally, financially or sexually abuse the family. As the mother leaves home to work she leaves her children at the mercy of the relatives and a host of trouble can emanate from one painful incident like rocks ricocheting off a wall.

Generations may suffer because a man was humiliated and mistreated by a 'master' who ridiculed everything about him and totally eroded his sense of worth. From that time of his life may arise attitudes towards authority or hatred of any one different from him, or a desire to impose his own brand of authority over the people he should love and care for. A sense of self-hatred might affect this man to the point where he dislikes anything that reminds him of what he was ridiculed about. I know there have been studies done which show the impact of slavery, discrimination and other practices that leave the oppressed person hating the thing that has led to the oppression be it a gender issue or a racial issue. For example some black people may end up doing all they can to adopt whiteness and if they can underplay their blackness not because they hate being black necessarily but in part because it is the blackness that has led to their oppression, so they deride food that can link them to blackness and they despise cultural aspects of blackness. They consciously or unconsciously blame the thing that makes them unique because some person somewhere despised them for being different. Yet regardless of how fluent and perfected your English or other Western language accent might be, it does not affect your external expression and presentation of who you truly are.

A man's pain could be the bad teacher he unleashes on his children imparting on to them his own warped views of society, his own views about the future; his own understanding of what is right or wrong. His sharing of his pain can become a major shell from which his own children emerge. His ways of dealing with his pain could be the source of pain for those who come in contact with him. If he doesn't deal with it, a situation emerges where an abused becomes the abuser and the abusive cycle repeats again and again.

Growing up I observed one of my relatives who was very harsh and unyielding in her views and in her ways. She had experienced disappointment as a young woman and this shell totally darkened her future. Because one man hurt her, she became a bitter, unyielding, unforgiving person and even her physical health was affected by this. She was let down by one man, she was disappointed and that became a major shell whose influence she never really managed to escape for life. Because of the let-down, her attitude towards life, men and marriage changed and became quite warped. Because of that incident also her heart became hardened. She found it difficult to forgive. She kept a record of what everyone did to her; she became a terror to the very people who sought her love, comfort and understanding. She became judgemental and analysed everything people said to catch them out. Her pain which happened possibly before I was born nevertheless affected my life as she became a source of terror for me and others. Instead of the love I thought I would get from her, there was condemnation, criticism, judgement and suspicion.

I couldn't do anything right and she freely shared her bitterness over what had happened to her in her youth. I was already dealing with stuff I didn't understand and this relative's apparent dislike of me simply became another shell for me to contend with, unable to crack it or escape because of family politics. Her disappointment and pain didn't just affect her. Because she never addressed them, she passed or tried to pass her views onto everyone else. Innocent people suffered because someone let her down and she never took time to forgive that person and everyone else that she had locked up in her grudge bag. How sad though to die never having forgiven and never having accepted that the past is gone and relegating it to the grave it deserves. How sad to end up with physical ailments caused by your own attitude eating you up inside causing disease and sickness and making people avoid rather than embrace you.

In a perverse way I am thankful that I wasn't one of her favourite people. Because of this, I never really took too much notice of her beliefs. If we had been close then maybe she could have influenced me to feel like she did, to hate and despise men like she did and to loathe relationships like she did. She became physically ill and I believe part of the illness was caused by what ate her up emotionally and spiritually. The impact of her major shell spanned more than 40 years and scarred her for life even as it fragmented into anger, bitterness, a failure to forgive, a judgemental attitude, a cutting sarcasm and a critical attitude towards people in general.

A person who has suffered from some form of abuse as a child may struggle with trusting people. Because of this they may have exacting standards which no one can attain and so they repel rather than draw people to them. The person may develop a suspicious or paranoid nature where they see everyone as out to get them. I know this from my own personal experience. It becomes difficult to accept love and kindness because you think nobody can possibly be nice without some nasty ulterior motive. When people offer to help you, you cannot accept their help because you question the authenticity of their charity. So even though the abuse may have happened a long time ago, if unchecked it can continue to send its mini-tremors into your future.

People whose parents neglected them financially can also become financially irresponsible. Nobody taught them to be caring and to provide for their families so they may unwittingly emulate even the parent they despise. Alternatively they could be so keen to overcompensate for what they didn't get that they become over-permissive parents who give in to their children's every whim turning them into spoilt brats rather than people of sound character. It all starts from the shell of neglect but from it future generations can be affected and their lives destroyed by the little shells being spewed out of the major one.

This is one of the reasons why issues in the past cannot be ignored or just left to their own devices. One may think that because they are not happening now then they can be ignored. Unfortunately traumatic events tend to blaze a trail through the lives they have happened to and they cannot be ignored, they have to be recognised, exposed and dealt with so that you can move on into an uncluttered future.

See what you make of this statement:

> *When you meet a person who is stuck in their past, it's like encountering stagnant water, there's an unpleasant smell in the atmosphere...* (Dr Ramson Mumba Facebook post 25th October 2012)

Bitterness and anger have the stench of a putrefying wound. It's that horrid mixture of life and death, life and decay in one place, it is an unpleasant surprise. It's not easy to love people and also condemn and judge them. It's not pleasant to claim to love someone and hit them and shout at them daily. It's an unpleasant combination of things. It's the paradox of trying to live in the present while using the past as a reference point. The past is supposed to be in the past while the present is your here and now. Lot's wife became an ineffective lump of salt (Genesis 19:26) because she couldn't look forward preferring instead to look back. But the word says that we are not of those who draw back to perdition (Hebrews 10:39). We look instead to Jesus who is both the author and finisher or perfecter of our faith (Hebrews 12:2), our healing, our deliverance, our wholeness.

Trying to move forward into the future, while also holding on to the grudges of the past and the anger and bitterness emanating from what happened to you, simply will not work. You may be making one step forward and four back, wondering why you are not reaching your destination. The future is there and available to you but your painful past is not welcome and it knows it so it drags you and weighs you down, prohibiting you from reaching your place of destiny. It's like when bullies snatch an object from one child and do all they can to stop him getting it back; it's a nasty form of teasing which is funny only to the bully.

There is nothing acceptable or right about colonialism or abuse. A colonial mind is wrong regardless of whether it is in a black, white or any other body. It is wrong if it leads to you walking around insecure with your head bowed down hypocritically deferring to people who have not earned the right to call the shots in your life. It is wrong when you walk around with a massive chip on your shoulder because of what 'they did to me'. A colonial mind-set is wrong if it gives you unearned, unjustified authority, power and privileges based purely on melanin levels. As long as shards of the colonial shell still draw blood in those it impacted, that means that the shell has yet to be crushed and ground and the resultant dust disseminated to the proverbial four corners of the earth.

So whether it's the main shell or the mini shell, you have to find a way of ditching them so that you can reach for the future God has in store for you. The main shell may be in the past but the mini shells run alongside you reminding you of what happened, affecting your relationships, tarnishing your character, weighing you down so that you have no strength for the things that matter, the things you should be focussing on, dimming your vision of what is important continually riveting your sight back to the past.

The cycle needs to be broken. The mini shells need to be crushed and rendered ineffective and powerless over your life. Deny them the power to impose the control of your past over your here and now.   Determine to embrace a future that if filled with God's best for you.

Chapter 6
Fake healing vs. the real deal

Some people walk around looking or rather appearing to be okay while they are dying inside. They have mastered the art of deception. They act as if all is well and smile correctly, laugh and talk correctly and they have sussed out the language of the healed. Yet the truth is that they have for whatever reason not allowed themselves to heal. Or maybe they have not had the opportunity to heal. One day something happens and they explode like a frozen pop bottle and everyone around them is left smeared with nasty stuff wondering what it is they just witnessed. It is a fake healing that has been exposed.

One thing that took me a long time to realise is that just because I don't consciously think about what happened in my past does not mean that I am over it or that I am now healed of it. For years I convinced myself that I was okay and that I was strong and had put everything in the right place, and I was doing all the politically correct things. But little things would happen and trigger inexplicable tears or anger. Someone would make an innocent comment and to me it would become a major issue. There seemed to always be something festering just under the surface. I was easily hurt, easily discouraged, easily put off people, easily affected by things people did. Watching television was a funny experience too as there were some things I couldn't watch even if there was no violence or explicit sexual stuff. They triggered things I couldn't explain in me. Even animals killing other animals had me terribly upset. Yet on the exterior all was well and because I am a strong person a lot of the time it is that strength which kept me going but times of crumbling were too frequent for my liking and I believe that maybe that strength stopped me from realising that I needed help sooner.

True healing does not leave areas of our hurt untended. It behaves like the word of God which is sharper than any two-edged sword and penetrates even to dividing soul and spirit, joints and marrow and also judging thoughts and attitudes of the heart (Hebrews 4:12). It goes deep into every aspect of our lives exposing areas that are still sore, still tender, still in denial, still blaming, still refusing to take responsibility, still building protective walls, still angry, still bitter, still judging and still fearful. True healing is not intimidated by finger clicking attitude nor is it bothered by being showed the hand. It goes where none dare and it fights all aspects of evil that deny us true forgiveness and deny those who hurt us true forgiveness. True healing is like love, it wants the whole person to itself, it won't share you with your issues, it totally wipes out anything that is not right and that keeps causing you pain. Partial healing is not good enough because it means that there are areas of your life that are still in pain and in despair. Healing stakes a claim on you fully, lock, stock and barrel.

A tough aspect or facet of healing is forgiveness. This is also one of the hardest things to do when someone has hurt you or abused you. It's not easy to forgive. One of the reasons we refuse to forgive sometimes is because we want the people who hurt us to suffer. We feel that if we forgive them they haven't paid for what they did and they have in effect won. We tend to fail to see that as long as we haven't forgiven we are in fact suffering twice too because the refusal to forgive means that we cannot bury the issue and lay it to rest. It means that we have to keep the issue on the fore of our thoughts and lives.

Forgiveness is like a funeral. It hurts to do it but it has to be done. If not the issue begins to decay and stink. Find a way to bury the issue and leave it in the cemetery. Don't go back to put flowers on that grave, in fact let the funeral parlour people conduct the funeral in your absence so that you don't even know where the thing is buried. It's not a loved one, don't visit it.

When you have been injured and have a wound you need to get it treated. It may need stitching up, it will definitely need some cleaning up and it will need some kind of balm, salve or dressing to help the healing process. You can't ignore it and just leave it to heal itself especially so if it is a deep wound. I never thought a wound could go so deep that it reached the bone, nor did I ever imagine that a wound could be so deep that it has to be packed with stuff to help it heal. But there are wounds that become so deep they uncover aspects of us that should never be exposed. They reach so deep that they affect emotions, character, habits, lifestyle and the very essence of who a person is. When a person feels like they have nothing to live for they have a wound reaching to the core of who they are. The longer the wound is left untended the deeper, the more painful, the smellier, the more crippling it becomes. If this is where you are, healing becomes imperative. You have to seek true healing and stop using plasters which can't really help because the wound is now too big and too deep.

Although the physical scars from the abuse you suffered may have healed, there are others that still need to be attended to. They won't heal on their own and if left untreated they will become septic and will cause complications. As a result, they need to be stitched or smothered in a salve and attended to not just once but over and over till they are fully healed. Whatever bandages are used have to be changed regularly, the wound cleaned and dressed again until total healing is achieved. The help you get will hurt as you explore areas of your life you prefer to hide. Each time you expose the wound for a fresh dressing it will hurt again but that is positive and constructive pain, it is pain that leads to healing, it is necessary pain. Specialist practitioners who know how to treat sores and wounds may be needed, just like you may need to speak not just to your friends and family but counsellors, pastors, and other people who can help you and dress your wounds and anoint them till you are free.

Your task is to take the wound to the people that can treat it, people that are able to see the wound and not pass out but they will look at it and probe around to check its depth then do whatever is needed to make it better. They will ask you to return for further treatment till you are healed. They are experienced enough to see that your wound is deep and that it will take time for the layers of it to heal. So they won't try to do everything in one session but will give each part time to heal and to be bound together again.

I know that there are times I have been in church and a message has been preached which really helped me. I left feeling lighter, feeling that I could now cope with certain issues and feeling good about myself. I have over time realised that something has actually happened and things are looking up. I have then listened to another message another time and it seems to be scraping off painful scabs, it hurts to listen to it, it exposes things I thought I had dealt with yet as the word is spoken tears have streamed down my face and I have realised that there are still aspects of what I was dealing with which need attention. This has happened several times and I have found myself becoming stronger, facing issues with less drama and trauma and definitely less tears. The healing wasn't instant. It was a process which covered, uncovered, cleaned, applied ointment, covered and then returned and started again. But because I have gone through it, I can truly say that Jehovah Rapha has done it for me, he has healed me.

It makes sense to me when I read Deuteronomy 11 from verse 18 that the process of being helped by the word if you are a Christian is not necessarily instant. You have to:

- ✓ Fix the word in your heart
- ✓ Fix the word in your mind
- ✓ Tie the word as symbols on your hands
- ✓ Bind the word to your forehead
- ✓ Teach it to your children 24/7
- ✓ Write the word on your doorframes
- ✓ Write the word on your gates

It would appear that there is need for continued reading and access to the word that heals, not a one-off exposure to it but a concerted effort to keep it before your eyes so that it can do a complete work repetitive and on-going healing. Do whatever it takes to be healed; you owe it to yourself and to your family.

There are some things you are too close to for you to be able to see and analyse clearly. You need the eyes of another to help you see and also to correctly break down the issue into its components without the emotional entanglement of personal pain and relational loyalties. You may need someone who does not know you personally and does not know the abuser so that they can help you wade through the issue itself and everything that has grown from it in your character, in your attitude towards people and in every other way. They will need to disentangle you from the bits of the shell still sticking to you causing pain and irritation. They need to be detached enough not to just sympathise but to really work on each aspect of your life that was affected by what happened to you. They may need to help you face and address your own anger issues that may have arisen from the fact that you were raised by an angry and abusive person. They may need to help you acknowledge and deal with substance misuse which may have come up because you were trying to find a way to forget what happened to you. Maybe they may need to help you deal with an issue of promiscuity or lack of trust, or fear of commitment, or some paranoia which have all stemmed from sexual abuse. The main issue is that you can't just hope that the pain will go away that your life will change on its own. You have to face it head on. You have to seek help.

My brother-in-law passed away a few years ago. He was the only person who realised that I needed help and he decided to give it the way only he could, straight-up! Most people can see that you have problems but they will either talk about you behind your back without ever making the effort to help you or even to admonish you in any way or they will act as if there is nothing wrong. Well this particular brother-in-law had no such qualms. He called me and gave me some home truths about the direction my life was taking. He could sense the anger and the bitterness and even though he didn't know the full cause or reason for them, he knew the course my life was heading would only lead to more pain and more bitterness.

So he told me what I didn't particularly want to hear but what turned out to be the beginning of a protracted process of healing. I didn't want to be told that I was destroying myself. I wanted pity and sympathy. He knew I didn't need those and that I needed healing not a loving but destructive caress. I am so thankful for him and for his tough love. I wish someone had said what he did to me sooner, but maybe I wouldn't have received it. Truth on its own can break you but when truth is laced with love and with grace it brings true healing, that is my experience and I pray that you will have people in your life who can speak the truth in love.

In summation then let me reiterate that you need to be healed. I can't over-emphasise that. You cannot continue on the path of hurt, pain, bitterness, shame, blaming and all the host of negative and confusing emotions currently assailing you. This is your life; you need to live it free of the baggage you have carried all this time. Time to off-load.

Chapter 7
Forgive yourself and them

One of the things I hated with a passion growing up was injections. Even when I had children I couldn't take them to the doctor or clinic and watch someone sticking a needle into them. The only reason I took them for their vaccinations was because I knew how important it was. My fear and discomfort were outweighed by what my children got; protection from child killer diseases and the build-up of immunity against conditions that could and still do kill children and adults. I knew it was good for me and for my children to have those injections and regardless of how terrified I was I had to look away and let it get done.

Forgiveness can be like that. We don't always want to do it because we think it takes away the upper hand we have when we hold something over somebody. Forgiveness can be one of the hardest things to do when you feel that your anger and pain are justified. It is hard to acknowledge that you must forgive someone who did not have any consideration for you and was so selfish they thought only of themselves and ignored the impact of their actions on another. Yet as we look at Christ on the cross at that moment of excruciating pain while the crown of thorns dug into his head and the pain of his body weight born on the nails that attached him to the cross, while the memory of the humiliating journey he had just undertaken was fresh in his mind, he still asked the father to forgive his murders, his tormentors and mockers. If he could do that, none of us has been hurt to the same extent and so we can ask him for the grace to forgive those who have wrongfully used and abused us.

If someone abused you sexually, physically or emotionally or in any other way, you may think that all you need to do is forgive them but sometimes you need to forgive yourself as well. This is not to say that you are to blame for their actions but sometimes what they did to you may have changed your attitude to life, to God and to other people. Your actions since then may have been laced by the anger or bitterness resulting from what happened. You may have put your life on hold by zeroing in on the past, refusing to let it go and move on. As a result, you need to forgive yourself and you also need to ask God to forgive you so that you can move on with your life.

This is a difficult aspect of the healing process. Yet it's also a crucial one. You are responsible for your own life and you have the power if you want to use it to change it with each day. The pain from your past can be dealt with if you allow God to heal you. The things you have done as a result of what was done to you can be forgiven because sometimes it is these more than the original abuse that can destroy your life. It is your own anger that can cause you to become a violent person who hits someone and causes irreparable damage. It could be your misuse of alcohol that causes you to drive under the influence and have an accident which affects other people. It could be your bitterness that causes you to neglect even your own children because you have not learned to love and care and show your feelings so that your children then experience neglect but this time it is you that has become neglectful and abusive.

If you were raised in a home where one or both parents were physically abusive, this will have had an impact on you. By abusive I refer to parents who hurt you out of anger, adults who hit you breaking limbs, bruising, scarring or causing any kind of physical injury. They dealt with you in anger and violence and because that is what they did that may be your only reference point for family. All you know all you connect to being in a family is being abused and being beaten or shouted and yelled at. You don't know any other way; you don't know that love teaches better than abuse and that your mouth can actually release what the bible in Proverbs 31 refers to as the 'law of kindness'. No one ever spoke to you kindly so it's unfamiliar territory. But that is not your fault nor is it right just because the adults in your life did it. Don't perpetuate their failure by allowing it into your future. Reflect on how you felt when they hit you or shouted at you and determine never to do that to someone else, particularly not your children.

Whether the abuse aimed at you was neglect or it was verbal abuse or emotional abuse it still caused harm. If the grown-ups who should have loved you did nothing but shout, yell and speak to you angrily or they called you names and never had a nice, encouraging word to say to you, that is also their fault, not yours. They were the adults and they should have known better. You deserved better and even though you didn't get it, it doesn't mean that you should be like them. You are better than that. Surround yourself with people you can learn from, families and role models who can show you what your parents may not have been able or willing to show you. Be the one that cuts the ribbon or shackle of abuse, be the first one to refuse to be the next rung in a lineage of abuse and pain.

The abuse may have been sexual. This means that some adult decided to introduce you to adult acts that you shouldn't have even known about at that time. They decided that instead of having sexual relations with another adult they would force themselves on you instead. So from a young age you were sexually aware. You may not have known the meaning of the things you felt. You started thinking sexually because of what had happened to you and you had nothing to preserve so maybe when the opportunity to sleep around came you felt that it was okay to do so, after all what could you lose again?

Whatever type of abuse you suffered may have made you live with fear, guilt, shame, anger, bitterness and other negative feelings that may have turned you into an angry and bitter person or maybe a promiscuous person as well. Maybe you ended up hurting other people the same way you were hurt or you began to shun intimacy. Maybe you became an overprotective parent or you couldn't trust anyone any more. Each person deals differently with what happened to them. Some seem to cope well and be resilient. Others become broken vessels straight away and struggle to survive. Yet they all need healing and help and if they stoically carry on unaided, a breaking point still manifests itself and it is not always pretty to witness or experience.

Take time look at yourself and see what you have become because of what you went through. Decide to be the one who breaks the cycle the one who refuses to perpetuate the cycle of abuse. Face it, deal with it and forgive yourself for whatever fireworks exploded from that core of hurt and pain caused by the actions of people who should have known better and who should have been protecting you.

The problem with guilt, bitterness and anger and all these other things is that they damage you and not the other person, they are not good bed fellows and you have to get rid of them. Yes the other person hurt you but the bitterness is in you not them, it's eating away at you not at them so you also need to deal with it and get rid of it. I learned this the hard way. In your heart you wish for all evil to befall the people who hurt you but it appears that the more you wish it the fatter they become, the more their lives seem to progress and prosper. It's pointless wishing bad things on people, you become a blesser instead because it is not in your nature to curse or harm. The best thing you can do for yourself is to give them up to God, let him deal with them in whatever way is best in his eyes.

You have to forgive yourself because maybe you have been using alcohol or drugs to dull the pain of your memories. Maybe you know that you are not doing the right thing because your past has been haunting you and diminishing your self-worth. Maybe you have been having relationships to hurt other people as you were hurt or you have been rescinding on your vows because you have trust issues. Whatever plethora of negative issues have exploded out of the hurt from your past need to be nipped in the bud and dealt with as well so that you don't suffer multiple hurts and continue 20 or 30 years after the abuse to be hurt by it.

I don't know of anyone who would expect you to become best friends with your abuser or to suddenly want to hang out with them. But I also know that you still need to let go of what happened. The issue of forgiveness is sometimes very difficult for a wronged person to deal with because they have been hurt and they may feel like they want to avenge their pain. Unfortunately, the more they hold on to the past the more they suffer for it. Bitterness and anger have teeth and they nibble and eat away at the person carrying them. You are the one who has a bagful of stuff you are lugging around. The other person is continuing to live their depraved life. You need to offload and leave that bag where it can't slow you down anymore.

So hard though it may be, you have to forgive the person who hurt you. You have to garner the strength it takes to do the unexpected, maybe even the abnormal. People expect you to remain angry. Do the opposite, forgive and move on. Let God be the one that avenges you. Focus on rebuilding what another sought to destroy: your life and your future. Value your life so much that you select what is allowed into it, and make sure anger, unforgiveness, bitterness and all the rubbish dished out by whatever shells you escaped from has no place. Each time any aspect of the painful past comes, lock the doors, change the locks, deny it access.

I love this verse, it directs us to the things we should focus on, and it guides us on our compilation of a guest list for what we invite into our lives:

> *Finally, brothers, whatever is true, whatever is noble, whatever is right, whatever is pure, whatever is lovely, whatever is admirable--if anything is excellent or praiseworthy--think about such things* (Philippians 4:8 NIV).

So your mind, your thoughts need to direct your actions towards things that are true, noble, right, pure, lovely, admirable, excellent and praiseworthy. Refuse to invite things that are painful, sad, angry, vengeful, judgemental, unforgiving, bitter, resentful or shameful. The former guest list will bring healing with it; the later will perpetuate and accentuate your problems. Choose the former and be healed.

Take comfort from these words by a survivor of a concentration camp who referred to what he faced and dealt with as 'the exceptionally difficult external situation' and noted that it 'gives man the opportunity to grow spiritually beyond himself' (Viktor E. Frankl. 2004 Man's search for meaning. Rider London p 80). You are still here; you are stronger than you thought you could be and what you have survived has given you strength you didn't know you had. The fact that you are still alive means you have overcome a huge hurdle, you refused to die, so you still have a future and I know that with God's help you will be better, much better than just okay.

Love or 'love'

©Farikanayi 5th December 2012

The paradox orchestrated by abuse

A father 'loving' you like you shouldn't be loved

While also loving you with a father's love

Can the two cohabit can he 'love' and love

The paradox cemented by a violent parent

How can you be nurturing what you are hurting

How can a parent's arms bring comfort to a child

When said parent is the origin of the distress

How then does a child understand God's love

Her confused mind cannot grasp the purity of his love

Nor that he is the definition of unselfish love

Her reference point is love that is tainted by 'love'

Chapter 8
Expect a good future

If you are a Christian, or even if you are not but you want to believe in someone who loves you and cares enough to want to work with you and ensure that both your present and future are not muddied by what happened in the past, then please read Isaiah 60 and find in its paragraphs promises and realities that can be yours if you receive them and believe in the one who has dedicated them to you.

Let's explore just a handful of these wonderful words of encouragement and hope as they speak that life will seep into what may have been a dead situation. Be eager to move on, to be led by God into a place of healing and peace, into a place where you are the star of the show and where he stands by cheering you on, encouraging you, telling you how precious you are and how truly wonderful he knows that you are. Let him show you just how good the future can be and just how dead the past is.

Imagine being in a situation where someone loves you and does something special for you each day. Imagine them waking up each day planning to surprise you with their love, planning to love you with their words, their actions and their attention. Imagine being secure in the arms of someone you can trust fully, someone who is faithful, who will never cheat on you or let you down, someone who will never hurt you. Multiply that love and security a million plus times and it still won't be as good or as special or as amazing as the love God has for you and for me. He wants the best for us; in fact he offered and still offers us his very best. Isaiah 60 highlights some of his love language, some of the sweet whisperings he makes in your ear and in mine to reassure you and me of his unmatchable love.

What I treasure about Isaiah 60 is the fact that it is an interactive portion of scripture. It highlights a loving father interacting with his child, and that is you and that is me. He knows his child intimately, every detail, the good, the bad and even the ugly. He knows the bitterness, the anger, the fear, the disappointment and everything that this child has done and also what others may have done to the child. Yet even as he knows all this, his love is not diminished, if anything it burns even stronger as he talks to us through these verses.

Isaiah 60 addresses the past and its pain. For example it refers in verse 2 to the darkness covering the earth, also covering his child because his child is in that earth. He knows that there are times his child can barely see clearly when pain shrouds his vision and shame blurs her sight. Yet he doesn't encourage them to wallow in self-pity or to remain in the place of darkness. Instead, he reminds them of who they are and of the fact that darkness is in the past, their portion is light and it is available to them so that they can see clearly and make good decisions and sound choices. He speaks about the reality of what may be around his child then uses the connective 'but' to show that there is an alternative way of living. His child does not have to remain in that darkness, in that place of mediocrity and guess work.

In verse 15 a reference is made yet again to the past. God knows that his child may have been forsaken, rejected, disliked, hated, abused and misused. Yet he comes through with promises of what he will do. He brings reassurance of the end of the experiences of the past. He reminds his children in verse 14 that even though they may have been oppressed at one time he will cause not just the oppressors, but the sons of the oppressors to bow. Generational recompense!

There is no time limit to God's goodness. This gives me such hope, knowing that just because something horrible may have happened a long time ago does not mean that my recompense or God's vengeance on my behalf is gone. I can claim what generations before me were deceived out of, or short-changed in wages or whatever it is that the thief did to take what he had no right to. So if my peace, innocence, wealth, joy, health, inheritance or anything else that was mine was stolen from me, God is still my recompense and he will make sure that Joel 2:25 is real for me. He will restore to me and to you whatever may have felt like it was chewed off you by the various locusts, cankerworms, palmerworms and caterpillars. God is our recompense. What was taken in the past will be restored in good measure, pressed down, shaken together and running over (Luke 6:38). Don't hold on to the munching caterpillar; don't keep looking at the damage it caused. Look to the one who promises that your now and your future will be more glorious than your past (Haggai 2:9).

Verse 18 reassures us of the end of violence if that is the shell we have crept out of. Maybe some bully has been physically abusing you and you have not found a way out. Believe what the word says; claim the end of the violence you have suffered. Don't become a perpetuator and perpetrator of the violence inflicted on you. Be the one that draws the end line.

Destruction and ruin are not your portion. God's desire for you is a peace which people around you cannot understand as it guards your heart and your mind (Philippians 4:7) even in the midst of turmoil and turbulence in your life. He wants the violence and the ruin to be in the past you don't even look back to. He wants your here and now to be so good that you don't even remember the past. He wants to heal you fully so that your life preaches to those still going through what he has delivered you from as you reassure them also that God will make and makes all grace abound towards them (2 Corinthians 9:8) and that his grace is sufficient for them (2 Corinthians 12:9) as it has been for you and for me.

Verse 17 is another place of promise referring to God moving us from a painful or lacking past to a present and a future which is better than the past we have escaped from. It is almost as if He is upgrading us from the mud to the palace, from hurt and pain to a place of rest and peace. Where we were weak and common he is promising strength and quality. He says in verse 20 that our days of sorrow will end. They have a timespan and have now reached the end! It has never been his intention for us to remain in the same place we were when we were hurt, abused, misused or in any way disadvantaged. He wants even our confessions to change as we realise that we are not who we were, we are who he says we are.

So we know we are the redeemed of the Lord (Psalms 107:2) and so we say what we expect, in agreement with his word. We may be feeling weak in relationships, in our physical bodies, in our finances or in our walk with God but he expects us to know that what we feel is not our reality. We may be feeling weak but in reality we are strong (Joel 3:10). Our lives must improve not stagnate, plateau or deteriorate.

I thank God that he doesn't just want us out of the painful or shameful past. He is clear about his expectations for our future. Isaiah 60 highlights a whole collection of words and phrases showing what he promises us. Let's explore a few aspects of our Abba Father's love language:

There is a definite promise of restoration, of what was lost being returned, of families reconciling, children returning to their parents. In the first verses there is also the reassurance that when he does this it won't be in secret. Your pain and shame may have happened and been perpetuated in secret but his restoration and recompense is in the open for all the world to see as it says in Psalms 23 that he will prepare a table before you in the presence of your enemies, in the presence of the issues and the people who may have wished you harm, those whose words shaped your life turning you into a timid and insecure child, those who hurt you till you no longer had any self-worth thinking that it is your lot to be someone's punch-bag. When he turns your life around, it won't just be in the local news, it will be known far and wide that the Lord has been good to you; the impact will not just be in you but your children and generations to come.

Then of course there are promises of his presence, of Jehovah-Shammah being present in our lives, being there with us, refusing to leave us or to forsake us. He really is a loving father and one who sticks by you and is there for you if and when you need him.

Earlier on I mentioned the fact that Isaiah 60 is an interactive scripture. It's not just about God speaking and promising certain things but it is also about him spelling out his expectations of us. As in verse 4 where he says: 'Lift up your eyes and look about you'. He knows that pain and shame bow our heads, making us look down so that even if good things are happening we can't see them because our eyes are cast down. He knows then it's not just about him changing our lives and our surroundings and environment. It is also about us shifting our focus from the ground to him, to the things he is doing and those he has already done. In verse 18 we are to call our walls Salvation and our gates Praise. This is not something for someone to say about us, this is our responsibility being spelt out. We name the places around us; we speak who we are and who we become. There is an expectation of our participation in what God is doing; we take ownership by taking an active interest and taking part in what is happening.

I know from my own past that I felt as if the world owed me something. People were supposed to know that I needed them and I needed their help. It never really occurred to me that I was a bit of a wimp and that each person is responsible for themselves not for me. Sometimes when stuff has happened to you your eyes can't look out anymore; you become so self-centred that you become a pain to the people you love and who hopefully love you too. But God says that we are the ones that determine what our walls and what our gates are to be called. We have a responsibility to ourselves, to our families and to the people around us. If we keep on looking inwards, we can't see the opportunities presented to us.

You may wonder why it is important for us to call and name our lives in a particular way. Think back to Genesis when God brought the animals to Adam to call them by particular names (Genesis 2:20). Whatever it is that he called them, they became. God has brought your life, your children, your spouse, your business and everything that touches you, to you to name them. They become what you call them. Call your children cheeky monkeys? That's what they become. Call your husband a fool? That's who you will live with. Call yourself poor? That is what you become. Call yourself the redeemed of the Lord who speaks and things happen? That's who you become. You have a lot of power in your hands, the power to alter whatever path your life is currently spiralling along.

One of the sad things about emerging from pain-inducing shells is the fact that you can become a needy person. It is almost as if whatever happened to you sapped you of strength and initiative. Even though maybe one person hurt you, your attitude can become magnified and exaggerated so that in the end the whole world owes you, the world has to pay the price for what that one person did. So you expect the world to pay your bills, to listen to you grumbling and complaining incessantly, to sympathise and empathise and to be there for you whenever you need them. Pain and hardship can make you a very selfish person as you seek your own and focus only on you. But regardless of what you have gone through it is still important to put things in perspective and to know that the world does not revolve or evolve around you. You still have responsibilities to yourself, your family and the people God has connected you with. Life still goes on and it is up to you to determine the quality you want to have. This means making some hard choices and it also means being honest with yourself. Expect the best for yourself and go after that but not at everyone else's expense.

James 4:2b says that some of the things we don't have are because we don't ask God for them. We keep quiet because sometimes we feel as if we don't deserve good things; we seem to assume that some people have ownership to good. But God expects us to speak and to ask for what we want him to do for us. Just as we ask for forgiveness we can also ask for healing and we can ask for wholeness. We can also ask him for people to become part of our circle who see the best in us and who care about us. God has given us free will, he cannot force himself on us, he responds to our prayers as we pray according to his word. Proverbs 3:4 tells me that I will have favour with men and with God. As I pray, I speak according to this scripture and so I can expect favour because I am speaking and praying according to his word. I am speaking what I want to happen in my life. I'm naming each brick that constructs my life; I'm making sure there is no accidental construction in my life. I'm whole, I'm healed, I'm gifted, I'm loved and loving, I 'm all things good according to the power at work in me (Ephesians 3:20).

Unfortunately, God is not moved by emotions, our erratic emotions. He is moved by his word and he responds to prayers that are made according to what he has said in his word. He is not a man that he should lie (Numbers 23:19) so if he made a promise in his word, he will honour that. We need to find it and take it to him, he will not allow that promise to return to him empty and unfulfilled but he will make sure that it is confirmed and accomplished (Isaiah 55:11). Our part is to make sure we know what has been promised us and to claim that.

So have expectations for good for yourself because that is also what he expects and he is so good that he also ensures that you don't have to accomplish it on your own, he is right there omnipresent with you and he will help you. Someone posted this on facebook on 4th December 2012 and I think it's a good quote with which to conclude this chapter:

> *'You can't start the next chapter of your life if you keep re-reading the last one'.*

Chapter 9
The pearly thread

Running alongside the nasty effects of the shells I emerged from has been a thread of my life, not always visible or evident but there regardless. This was my emergent faith, built up in a few Sunday school classes, strengthened through family devotion with parents who insisted on God living with us, and shaped along the way through erratic church attendance and a lingering love for gospel music. This was an unquestioning faith that I would live and that it would be well with me. This faith's fire was fanned into life at various stages in my life by people who became connected to me, some long term and others only for short spurts.

It is this thread of faith, not always my own, not always solitary that has brought me to the place where I can explore these shells without tears, oh okay, let me re-phrase that and say without too many tears. So I can explore the source of the pain, I can analyse the product of the pain and I can sift through the destruction it has caused. I can now do all this because of the tenacity of that thread of faith, because though unseen sometimes, though threadbare sometimes, it is there and it is not leaving. It has wound itself around the issues I have faced and dealt with. It has participated in lifting me up when I fell so low I didn't think I could rise again. It has clung on to me even when I didn't know it was still there. Its works have continued to speak, to connect me to God's word and to make me feel and sense the presence of one who has loved me and continued to love me even when all some would do was abuse.

The thread of faith has helped me see glimpses of good when everything was collapsing around me. This faith stubbornly refused to let me go, and it continued and continues to focus me on the lifter up of my head (Psalms 3:3), on the one that refused to let me keep walking looking down as if I don't deserve to look up and look at people straight in the eye.

Another really exciting thing about this thread of faith is the fact that I don't need to spin it on my own. Oh I am so grateful to God who knows me so well that he has put things into place in my life because he knows me and he knows my failings and my weaknesses. Faith according to the bible comes by hearing God's word (Romans 10:17). Now although there is an expectation for me to do something in this case hearing, the reality is that what builds up my faith or what adds to its growth is the word that those God has anointed to teach it say. I just need to sit down, turn on my cd player or go on YouTube and type in the name of a preacher I know speaks the word of God in truth and I need to listen to them and as I do so, my faith is strengthened, it grows to the point where I can now exercise it through linking it to action thus keeping it alive. So if I listen to a message on love and I hear and receive that message, I can then exercise my faith by loving where it has been difficult before. Faith convinces me that love is not in vain, that my love will make a difference in someone else's life, and that I should love anyway because the word of God says I should.

That has been such a tough lesson to learn. God's word doesn't change to accommodate me. It doesn't operate out of pity for me because that would be counterproductive. God's word is forever settled in heaven (Psalms 119:89). It has been spoken and it is what it is. God is not a man that he should lie (Numbers 23:19) and we cannot compare him to sons of men who repent, renege on promises, change their minds, lie and cannot always be trusted. God spoke, he made sure that his word was settled, un-shifting, not in any way like Reuben who is compared to water (Genesis 49:4). When the environment around it is very cold it freezes, as things warm up it melts. When the heat is turned on poof! It evaporates. No, God is not like that. His word is the same for everyone. He has already said we should love God and our neighbours (Matthew 22:37-40). He has already said that we shouldn't judge others lest we also be judged (Matthew 7:1). He has already spelt out the seventy times seven times we need to forgive (Matthew 18:22). His word requires my cooperation as I do what God says and as my faith is built up by that word.

I have to thank God for all the men and women out there who have made me realise that I am not inferior to anybody. They have opened up God's word and directed me to scriptures like Isaiah 49, 54, 43 which all tell me in no uncertain terms how precious I am to God, how important I am in his plan for my generation. I'm not an after-thought; I'm not a substandard creation. It really doesn't matter how hard someone tries to diminish who I am. My worth is not determined by people but by God, my creator, the lover of my soul and this word is already settled in heaven, it cannot be re-written by someone who wants to destroy my confidence.

This is so liberating. The only problem is that sometimes we so value the opinions of mere mortals and are hurt when that opinion keeps shifting and changing and when it is not complimentary. Who cares if someone doesn't like how you look? That's their opinion. I prefer to believe the Creator's opinion and he says that I am wonderfully and fearfully made (Psalms 139:14) that I am like a cornerstone (strong, purposeful) polished after the likeness of a palace (expensive, high quality, precious, useful, vital to the very existence of everything attached to me), that opinion expressed in Psalms 144:12 is what counts, not what someone else thinks and says.

When God looks at me he sees his son in me, he sees someone made in his own image. As I hear the word of God faith continues to grow and to remind me that I am not average or mediocre, I am gifted, I am skilled, and I am talented. Because of this I can go out and follow my dreams.

As that faith also strengthens, it tells me that my past is not my future and that regardless of how I started off, I can run the race of life and excel. Faith tells me also that I am a beautiful and desirable woman, I am not a reject, I am not ugly or dirty because of what happened in my past or because I don't fit someone's assessment or aesthetic standard. I no longer need to accept any relationship that is not in line with God's word. The man that will get me as his wife is one blessed dude, just like anyone I allow to cross the line into my inner circle. In me they will definitely and without a doubt get God's best. Not everyone will look at me and see what God sees. Some will be like the spies sent to spy the Promised Land (Numbers 13 -14). They will see with limited human sight. They will be challenged by the awesome work God has done to make me who I now am. Because of the lens they see me through, they will miss out on getting to know the wonderful person that I now am.

I like what 2 Corinthians 4: 7-10 talks about. It's such a faith building scripture as it shows what may have happened in the past and the final outcome for people of faith.

But we have this treasure in jars of clay to show that this all-surpassing power is from God and not from us. We are hard pressed on every side, but not crushed; perplexed, but not in despair; persecuted, but not abandoned; struck down, but not destroyed. We always carry around in our body the death of Jesus, so that the life of Jesus may also be revealed in our body (NIV).

How wonderful for us but so frustrating for the enemy that regardless of what he brings our way we are like cork that refuses to submerge under water. We keep coming back on top, we keep resurfacing, and we keep bobbing up to the top. Life's challenges, the battles we face, the difficulties that provide an onslaught or barrage on us don't have the power to keep us down or to keep us under. We serve an awesome God who planted in us that seed of faith, he made a deposit of it in me and it is a tenacious, hardy, strong and surviving faith. And I am grateful that this thread has continued to make its majestic and life-saving presence felt in my life. We take comfort from scriptures like Job 22:29, Proverbs 24:16 and Psalms 34:19. We keep bobbing back up to the surface.

Recently this thread of faith which also has a knack for recognising the places where the healing word is spoken connected me to a ministry where I have seen my past addressed, exposed, set in perspective and sent packing. I have had every aspect of my life hit with the flood-light of truth so that all the hidden and secret passageways couldn't continue to hide pain or accommodate fear and disappointment. Every excuse, every reason to bow down, every wound has been dealt with until as the dross fell off me I began to see myself as God has always seen me and intended that I should see myself. The areas of my life that were inaccessible to healing because they had not been uncovered and smothered in his healing balm were now tended both patiently and relentlessly until they too bowed to the superior wisdom and healing of God's unchanging yet living word. It is in this place that God has loved me and taught me to love, where he has connected me to people who see worth in me and value me not for anything other than the fact that I am who he says I am. I am thankful for the brook God has planted me in, healed and delivered me in, helped me in, loved me in and loved me in again.

Maybe what excites me the most is the fact that now that I am not focussing on the pain or the hurt, I can look out and see that there are hurting people out there that I can help. There are people who have experienced ten times the pain I have and whose lives are spiralling out of control faster than mine was. I couldn't see them before because my eyes could only see me; they were shrouded in pain and selfish concerns. Now that I can see clearly I can also see where I can help and where I can offer support.

In addition to just being able to see other people and their needs I can now also see myself more clearly. Where I only saw through pain tinted and bitterness tinged eyes, I can now see who I am, the gifts, the abilities and the talents in me. I can see that my life has a purpose which must be fulfilled and it cannot and will not be marred by my past. The following statement now begins to apply:

> 'A man who becomes conscious of the responsibility he bears toward a human being who affectionately waits for him, or to an unfinished work, will never be able to throw away his life. He

knows the 'why' for his existence, and will be able to bear almost any 'how'' (Viktor E. Frankl. 2004. Man's search for meaning. Rider London pp88-89).

When there is a purpose to live for, hardship cannot derail the focus you now have. Draw strength from the good you will do as you fulfil your destiny even though things have happened that tried to hinder and obstruct you in your race. I used to be discouraged when I couldn't give until I realised that giving has nothing to do with how much I have. There are things I can do even at a time when I don't have any money. There are ways I can still ensure that it is well with someone else. I don't have to be a millionaire to be a blessing. This is a lesson I felt the Holy Spirit teaching me. I have to start from where I am. I can share what I already have with another; I can combine a gift with two or three people and make something good we can then bless another with. When I do become a millionaire I will continue giving on a larger scale but the giving pattern has to start even from sharing the little bit I may have at present. I loved this lesson because it took my eyes away from me to others and it made me realise that I am actually blessed. That is what happens when you are in a place where that thread of faith is stretched and strengthened, in a good church where the preached word and the word you study and meditate on your own finds fertile ground in your heart and is stored there so that your life aligns with God's will (Psalms 119:11; Luke 6:45).

Let me conclude this section by referring to pearls. They are beautiful, expensive, sought after and one of the symbols of wealth, yet their beginnings are as humble as mine. They emanate in nature from an irritant, a grain of sand which lodges itself in an oyster. As the oyster covers up the irritant with nacre, a pearl is formed. It takes years for a pearl to form and for it to be harvested and used to make precious necklaces, rings and other jewellery. People pay a lot of money to buy what started off as a grain of sand, an aggravation, but God works in such a way that what was meant for harm becomes a beautiful, useful object gracing even the necks and ears of queens.

Dig deep in yourself and allow your eyes to see the nacre layering over the pain, the filth, the shame, the discouragement and whatever else the enemy may have brought your way to devalue you. God will take that irritant, that situation and deny it the power to cripple you. Instead, with his loving and tender care, he will make sure that by the time he is done with you; a pearl of great worth will emerge.

Eye has not seen nor has ear heard nor has it entered the hearts of man the things that God has prepared for you (1 Corinthians 2:9).

Just be expectant, God will surprise you with the finished product you never expected that you could become.

Chapter 10
Still here

I was talking to one of my friends the other day and listening to him cite some of the challenges he has faced and the difficulties he has walked through. I was touched by the fact that he acknowledged that it is God's goodness that has kept him. Everything that could go wrong has gone wrong for him yet God has continued also to show the rainbow of his love as it shines even through the darkest moments. I am grateful that my friend has not succumbed to despair but has held on to the faith that continues to keep him standing and serving his maker to this day. Many wonder how he has remained sane, how he appears jovial. But he knows who he has believed and so he is grounded.

Another friend went through different issues but whose potency and capacity to derail were just as strong and harsh as the one mentioned above. His life seemed to crumble around him as one thing after the other just seemed to go wrong and as challenges relentlessly threw their rocks at him. For a while nothing went right and life got as close to despair as it could. Yet during that time, in that phase of his life that is when our friendship was birthed and I grew to love and respect him as I glimpsed the strength of this man's faith, his determination to succeed and overcome, his unwavering reliance on the one true God and his constant aligning of his words with God's word. What a joy also to see that word begin to steer him from the mud to blessings in every area of his life. What a faith strengthener for me to see a life quite close up rising above the challenges and like David hitting each giant not with man's wisdom (although he has his fair share of that) but over and over with the word of the Almighty.

I celebrate my friends as I see them stand, begin and continue to reap the harvest of their faith as they stand in the middle of their confession and as Jehovah-Shammah, our ever-present God shows himself faithful again and again.

There is this paradox, a contradiction about life. In many ways it is both fragile and strong, both delicate and tough, both flimsy and hardy. A person can die from a blow to a particular area of their body, yet a person can be involved in a fight or be assaulted and their body badly beaten but they still stagger up and heal. A person can lose their mind as a result of bereavement or rejection, a painful incident which can totally alter their life, yet a child can be abused by an evil adult for years and bounce back and still become an excellent parent and citizen. Life can be weak or strong and sometimes it is difficult to understand why something that destroys one person strengthens another. I now know, for myself that faith and hope are powerful support mechanisms. Despair on the other hand, guarantees failure. The bible says that when hope is deferred when it cannot be pinned down to work in a given situation then the heart goes weary and gives up (Proverbs 13:12):

Hope deferred makes the heart sick, but a longing fulfilled is a tree of life (NIV)

Hope allows us to keep going; it is like a catalyst, like a voice in our ears saying;

'Come on now, this is not the end of you, there is something good just round the corner, I am not letting you quit, you are not on your own. Can't you see I am here with you, keep going, tomorrow will be better, this too shall pass, keep going, don't give up.'

And as long as that voice is speaking and you are actively listening to it, you can see the light at the end of the dark tunnel. But when even that voice is hushed, then despair will have won.

I know sometimes people don't understand what keeps me going, or what has kept you going in-spite of all you have had to deal with in life whether as a result of bad and poor choices or because of what others have done to you. Sometimes it is hard to even understand it myself. But one thing I do know is that God has not allowed me to quit, he has ensured that even in the toughest of times, even in the most apparently hopeless situations something has still happened to snap my head back up so that my sight remains connected to my help, to the lifter up of my head (Psalms 3:3). He will not allow me to be tempted beyond what I can bear (1 Corinthians 10:13), as long as I don't give up; he equips me to overcome the challenges. I try to be low and to get depressed and sad and usually I succeed for all of 30 minutes. For whatever reason God has put a happy trigger in me and I cannot remain sad, I cannot remain in despair or despondency. Part of it I now know comes from the name my parents gave me at birth. You can't be called 'Celebrate, be happy' and be sad. That name is a living prophecy which is pronounced each time someone calls my name, each time I respond to it, each time I write it down, Eish! I am a happy person because my parents made sure of it. Name your children wisely, that might be the only positive word being spoken daily into their lives.

Sometimes we focus so much on our pain and the hard times we have come through that we don't realise that we have actually come through. Psalms 23 talks about walking through the valley of the shadow of death and that is a powerful statement. Yes there was imminent death in the valley hence its name, no one can argue with the fact that things were bad. But further to that, it gives us the impression that we don't sit in the valley of the shadow of death nor do we stand still and become transfixed by the various shades of black and grey that make up the shadow. Instead we are in motion. If the valley is 100 metres long we start off with 100 metres in front of us but from the moment we take the first step, the length of the valley is reduced. We walk through it until there is 20 metres then 10 then two and in the end we emerge from the valley of the shadow of death. We don't die there, we walk through it.

That is the same situation a person who was abused or who emerged from whatever harsh shells encircled them. They didn't die there, they emerged and that is a very hopeful place to be.   Don't go back and find a comfortable place in the shell to sit there or lie down there. You have emerged, the shell has cracked. There is no more space in it for you, if you try to sit there it will poke and prick you with the shell remnants of pain and bitterness, fear and shame, unforgiveness and everything else that dwells in the shells. You are out of it, thank God and find a better place to be, a place of forgiving and being forgiven, a place of shalom where there is nothing missing or broken in your life. That is not found in the shell; you have walked through and out, now stay out. Celebrate the fact that you survived the shell, it can't encapsulate you anymore, you are here, you are alive.

A shell does not have the power to reconnect its fragments and swallow you back into it. If you find yourself still residing in a shell from which you already emerged, maybe you got some super-glue and you have been piecing the shell bits together. Leave the bits alone, the shell is not for you. You emerged. Now get on with life.

If you have never read this verse, read it now and allow God to speak to you through it:

> Lord, you have assigned me my portion and my cup; you have made my lot secure. The boundary lines have fallen for me in pleasant places; surely I have a delightful inheritance. (Psalms 16:5-6 NIV)

I believe that what this verse says is a crucial starting place for healing regardless of what shells you are stepping on so that you can crush them, their memory and their hold on you. It's a set of words which acknowledge the presence of someone much greater than myself and who is able to get involved in my life. The benefit of this is the fact that this someone is able and willing to give me the security I lost through focussing on the shells and the smells emanating from them dirtying my life.

As I read these words and I pray for a similar experience for you, I realise that regardless of how difficult the journey has been or how difficult it still is, there is one who is willing to take the healing effort from my own hands to his. I don't have to do this on my own, I don't have to heal myself, in fact I can't heal myself. So what he is doing is reinforcing to me that my lot is secure, he has assigned a lot and a portion for me and this is why I need to get my healing. The insecurity wafting up from the shells interferes with my lot. The inconsistencies in my behaviour due to pain, hurt and spasmodic recollections of the past which lead to outbursts of anger or words that hurt others also interferes with my lot. The fear clouding any relationship I attempt to get into also interferes with my lot. My lot is secure; it is not bitter or angry, neither is it hurtful or fearful. My lot is secure, established, grounded, firm, and unbreakable. That's a good place to be.

Let's explore this a bit more. When you secure your house and install an alarm system you are making it secure for you on the inside but you are also making it secure against external forces that want to come in. You build a strong and secure house to protect you and yours from external elements which you want to keep external. You don't want the snow drifting into your house or the rain washing your carpets for you. Those forces have to be kept outside. Imagine if you then destroy the alarm system from the inside, if you then destroy the house from inside. The alarm is not meant to protect you from you. It is meant to protect you from those out there who wish to harm you. Now the Lord makes our lot secure, he puts things in place for our good, but even though the lot is secure, we can make it insecure by continuing to walk in strife because of our hurt, our pain, our memories and maybe greatest of all our unforgiveness.

But reading this verse again we realise that there is a wealth of promises here but, as with most things in life we have a part to play, we have choices to make. God has already done his part; we need to connect with it by also doing our part. Unfortunately this is where we start having some casualties of faith. Some people want God to be their on-call worker, available at their beck and call. They complain when things don't work out and grumble if they don't get what they want straight away. God is supposed to be healing them, blessing them, protecting them and their families and making rain come when they want it to. Yet they don't seem to realise that the blessing is part of the covenant or maybe it is a result of the covenant, the two-way relationship we have with God where his grace is sufficient for us (2 Corinthians 12:9) and where we are expected to love. God always keeps his side of the covenant even to undeserving mortals but we are found to fall short many a time. We shirk on our responsibility and don't always hold up our end of the bargain.

We are also told here that we have an inheritance which is described as delightful. The places God expects us to settle in are cordoned off in pleasant ways. Putting this issue really simply, fear, self-doubt, anger, manipulation, bitterness, low self-esteem and all the nasty stuff that may still be rising up from the shells are not pleasant. As long as we are still allowing them into our lives we are denying ourselves, refusing to allow God to set our feet upon the rock in pleasant places. Some things simply won't co-habit. As with most things, we need to make a choice about which place we want to settle and which inheritance we want to claim. It's time to allow God to help you give notice to every shell, every fragment of the old shells, and every aspect of the shell that hasn't left yet, they all need to be served notice so that you can come into your real inheritance. You need to read the will and find out the extent of your inheritance then lay a claim.

Yet again, there is the expectation for our active involvement. The inheritance is there but it needs to be claimed and then it needs to be used wisely not only for our own benefit but for our children, our families, our neighbours, our community and our generation. We have the power to affect our times. The tools are there, the inheritance God has given us even as he presents us to display his splendour as it says in Isaiah 49.

2 Corinthians 5:17 is another super set of words that can take us from the history of shells to our delightful inheritance, but it also spells out something we need to do, something that is demanded of us. It talks about becoming a new creation when you are in Christ and that old things have passed away and that everything has become new. Pain is old, joy is new. Anger is old, love and peace are new. Harshness and nastiness are old but gentleness is new. Fear is old and boldness and confidence are new. Being aimless and dreamless are old; having a purpose to live for is the in thing. Whatever happened in the past happened but it is part of the past and it must not be allowed to shape the future. There is help when this transition is difficult to make. It still needs to be made. The old things cannot be allowed to remain.

Our task is to embrace the new and deny the old or rather reject the old.

What I am saying then is that I am still here. He has kept me. He has kept me in perfect peace (Isaiah 26:3) when it appeared like my whole world was out of kilter. Sometimes I look at my life and I wonder how I got here, I wonder how I managed to scale some of the mountains that littered my paths each time I thought I could take a breath in relief. I don't know how he has provided for me so that my children and I had food when we had no money with which to buy it. I don't know how he has kept my mouth filled with laughter so that no one looking at me would know what I was going through. I am here and I cannot attribute my presence to cleverness, to my family, to anything or anyone else other than simply the goodness and the graciousness of a loving father who has refused to let me go even when I just wanted to surrender and call it a day.

If I can be here after some of the things I have hinted at, believe me so can you. He will be with you through the trials and the turmoil. He will protect and shield you from danger that should have killed you. He will cover you with his love ensuring that underneath you are his everlasting arms (Deuteronomy 33:27). He will provide for you a cleft in the rock, a refuge and a place to run to and hide when the storms appear relentless. God loves you and no battle is too fierce for him to win for you, no army too great, and no issue too strong. Trust him, call on him, believe him, and give him the reigns of your life.

Kurt Carr sings a song called 'I almost let go'. It's a good song to listen to as it helps refocus your attention to what God can still do regardless of what the enemy may have planned. God has kept you, so you can't let go. You have a future he still wants to perfect if you will let him. Don't let go. The answer is nearer than you think and better than anything you ever imagined. You are still here.

Chapter 11
My reflections

One of the ways I have combated feelings of bitterness despair and anger is through writing poems about the things that have taken place in my life. I have had to destroy some of them because they were an expression of pain and anger and sharing them would have been perpetuating what I needed to get rid of. They may not pass any academic poetry standards but they became a useful and vital tool for my healing. They were useful for exploring the feelings and once these were open, I could then apply the healing ointment of forgiveness and move on.

Now what you read is no longer the bitter and angry ranting of a victim but expressions of a healed and healthy life that has acknowledged the amazing future awaiting her and has kicked the past back to the day and the year it happened and where it belongs. This is not to say that once kicked off that way that the past then stays there. Sometimes it sneaks in, other times you smell it and know that it is rearing its ugly head again. The kicking has to be an on-going process, don't allow it to return, kick it back and keep burying it if it excavates itself. Maybe in part this is what the scripture about working your own salvation with fear and trembling refers to (Philippians 2:12).

Be wise enough to recognise the symptoms of the past. Know the areas it has tainted in the past so that you can quickly sense it's presence before it even gets to a station near you. One scripture I have found really helpful says the following:

> *I can do everything through him who gives me strength (Philippians 4:19 NIV).*

I got to the point in my life where I doubted my intelligence, ability to make a sound decision, ability to survive or capability as a mother. I started second guessing myself in everything I did and of course this only compounded my low self-esteem and further diminished my own worth in my own sight. Being in a good church means you really do become equipped by the preached word and by the word you are encouraged to read for yourself as you lay up the word of God in your heart. I realised that I have super weapons in my hands to fire at any and all volleys being hurled by my past. I can speak the word and it will sort out whatever issues I am facing. When I feel insecure, incapable and as if I don't measure up, I speak that scripture and I know for sure I can do all things through Christ who gives me strength (Philippians 4:19). As the past tries to remain standing, I can counter it's presence with the word of God against which the past has no defence. It has no choice but to bow and scuttle back into the dark nether-regions from which it keeps trying to escape.

For me then, writing is a powerful healing tool that God has put in my hands. Some people drink or do drugs as their way of dealing with issues facing them. Some people hide, some sing. I write. Okay sometimes I also eat too many scones, but generally I write. I don't always write for an audience, some of the things I write are for my eyes only, for my healing. But I know now also that as I write, Isaiah 50:4 is real. My pen, my keyboard keys are all part of my way of speaking to you. I know that God has given me an instructed tongue and as I speak/write, I know that he will cause the words he has given me to heal and to bring strength to the weary, wisdom and clarity to someone who was struggling for a solution and answers if you just needed to know what to do.

Let the following pieces then both heal and encourage. Add your own story as you read and together let us encourage another and bring healing and health to them through the goodness we see God doing in our lives.

Yielding continuously to His healing

©farikanayi 5th April 2012

A truth floated into my consciousness today
Bringing tears to my eyes conjoined with understanding
Some of the things I have done
Been deeply rooted in memories forgotten buried deep

It was like a light shining in a dark place
Illumination the elusive never caught comprehended
Opening just that little bit more
What all these years could not apprehend could not grasp

As I prayed asking for God's help today
Pleading that every hidden sin be revealed exposed
Like a burst he clarified pointed it out
Forgive me Father heal me and help me also to forgive

The pain of unearthing cuts deep intense
But rather that and have my healing process begin
Than to keep it hidden revealing a little
I need my future free and uncluttered by the past Father

Surround me oh Lord in your embrace
As long as underneath are your everlasting arms
I can handle it Lord I need it over
Your banner over me is love in your love is my healing
So help me Lord let's work on this now
Let's unearth in gory detail let's lay it bare
Pour your healing balm on me Lord
I put my trust in Jehovah-Rapha the Lord my healer

Ask God to heal you enough to deal with what you discover about your past as you unearth it and expose it to his healing light.   Don't allow your past to keep surprising you, appearing at awkward moments, embarrassing you at unexpected turns. Ask God to help you retrace your steps so that you bury anything you haven't dealt with as yet. Unburied corpses stink up your present. The flies attracted to them invade your future. Whatever you do, ask God to be your constant companion on that journey.   He has the power to effectively bury it all with you and for you.

Till you yield to his healing

How can you feel shame
For the actions perversions of another
For adults catalysing your thoughts imaginations
To areas foreign and strange not yet in your radar
Bringing awareness of deeds thoughts from forbidden
lands

How do you make sense
Hating the activity with no reference point
Of rightness wrongness as fear sits on the throne
Adults using threats fear well cultivated power games
To demand silence coerce and ensure juvenile
participation

How do you shake it off
When your thoughts now directed by events
Outside your control but influenced by 'loved ones'
Parental eyes adult care should have protected shielded
But this became your reality it's now stamped as your
history

How do you now escape it
When innocence quickly snatched from you
Mirror reveals filth soiled second hand products
So you self-clean and present offer yourself in acts of
'love'
Haunting thoughts override and doubt cries out
'unworthy'

Can passage of time heal
Back to the mirror unchanged image filth look away
Cyclic repetition punctuated by shouts screams
'unworthy!'
Again you flee hands over ears blocking mockers eyes
shut
No efforts have healed accumulation of pain more shame
more hurt

How can you still feel shame
For the actions perversions of those evil others
If you don't yield to His healing submit only to His healing
Cycles viciously repeated persist shame shouts even
louder
Till you curl up in surrender and snuggle into His loving
healing embrace

Whatever pain and torment pervaded your life is not your fault. The adults who abused and misused you carry the blame and the guilt. Your responsibility is to seek healing, to find healing, so that your life can escape the tarnished cycles that will repeat until you break them. Be adamant that you need healing, persistent in your search for it, unrelenting in your acceptance of the right to live and enjoy life and hopeful in the knowledge that God can turn this and any situation around for your good. It is not your fault.

I should hate you

©farikanayi 26th June 2012

I should hate you
I really should be angry with you
I've earned the right to be bitter at you
Yet all I do is feel pity for you

I should still be crying
I should tell everyone I'm a victim
You could so easily have destroyed me
Yet I'm healed you see I'm strong

It may have taken a while
For pain buried deep subconsciously
To surface dogging my dreams my days
But now I recall I can deal with it

I could wallow in self-pity
Rehashing remembering reliving it
Many walked the path I trod many do
I have overcome your evil deed

If you still hurt and still cry
Turn snuggle into God's loving arms
Let his love destroy the pain the past
Dump pain ditch the victim victor

Laughing at a person who is tormenting you must infuriate but also confuse them. I love the scripture which says the following: 'You will laugh at destruction and famine, and need not fear the beasts of the earth'

145

(Job 5:22). Do what is not expected of you. Where you should be crying laugh instead! Where you are expected to die determine to live long and live strong. Abusers are part of the beasts of the earth, those who seek to cause pain and harm in innocent lives. Refuse to let what they did continue to affect you. Show them that you are made of sterner stuff. Don't hate them, forgive them, laugh at their antics and live a life that exceeds anything your past thought you could live. Don't hate. Love and live.

Hey past

©farikanayi 27th May 2012

My past thought he had so much power
That he could continue undeterred into my future

My past thought she had so much sway
That she could influence the course of what lay
ahead

My past thought it was still fearsome
Intimidating me into surrendering God's plans for me

My past thought he had subdued my life
Making me ineffective powerless to pursue my goals

My past had mistaken illusions of grandeur
Thinking it could hurt me now like it hurt me then

My past assumed she had omnipotence
Unaware He's greater with power to erase her off
me

My past thought he gave perpetual hurt
Oblivious of the healing power of Jehovah-Rapha

My past didn't know the power of etymology
That past means gone previous history already lived

Come on past respond wave goodbye
My future beckons God's plans present my destiny

I love knowing that God's plans for me are plans for good and not evil to give me a hope and a future (Jeremiah 29:11). His plans do not include or seek references from the past. They are about my here and my future. I love also that the glory of this house, this time of my life and the future God has mapped for me far exceeds whatever has been in my past (Haggai 2:9) my destination is for better not for worse than what I have seen or lived to date. Tell your past that it has already accomplished the best it can do. Tell it its ticket ends here, it has been denied the visa into your future.

The stains

©farikanayi 13th November 2012

The bleeding was stopped when she extended her hand
for her miracle
Yet onlookers may have seen the stains and still called
her unclean
Little did they know that the stains were not an illness
they were just stains
Just a reminder the evidence of her miracle of what He
did for her

Joseph's father saw his beloved son's blood-spotted coat
of many colours
He cried assuming the blood stains signified the death of
his adored
Little did he know that the blood he saw was just stains of
intended evil
That his son was on his way to an Egyptian palace to his
promotion

They saw the blood Jesus shed on the cross and went
home devoid of hope
The spilt blood mistakenly symbolising death failure
misplaced trust
They equated it to the end of their expectation ultimate
defeat of a saviour
Little did they know Jesus would arise in total victory over
death

Some may look at you today and all that is evident is the
scars from battles
In pity they see the stains and assume your defeat and
write you off
All they see is the confirmation of what you have been
through lived through
Little do they know you are walking into your place of
SHALOM

As you redirect the eyes of the world from your then to
your amazing now
Shift your eyes also to the plans for good He has
bequeathed to you
Grab hold of spiritual scissors snip off the sting of death
the stink of the past
You are a new creation He has dealt with your pain stand
in your victory

I read a post on Facebook (adapted from FB item posted by Fungai Matthew Benhura 12/11/12) that got me writing. It spoke about the stains on the garments of the woman commonly referred to as the woman with the issue of blood. People have a way of seeing us in past tense. For some reason it is difficult for their brains to move on from when we were ill, when we made a mistake, when we did something wrong. If we are not careful, we can see ourselves the same way people see us and that is in direct contradiction to how God sees us. He is not focussed on our pasts because he is a good shepherd and he is leading us instead to our green pastures as says Psalms 23. Realign your thinking to his, you are wonderfully and fearfully made, he loves you dearly and he delights in your success, prosperity and victory (Psalms 35:27)

Chapter 12
Highlights

Before I wrap this up, let me make a kind of summary of what I have learned.

➤ Looking back constantly in the physical hurts your neck. It also tampers with your vision because of the location of your eyes; you can't look back and see what's ahead of you. To see what is in the future one has to look forward, if you keep looking back you see what is in the past rather than what is in your bright future. Press your life's 'play' rather than 'rewind' button

➤ Many people continue to hurt because they keep looking at what happened. As a result, they keep rehashing the events and they keep reliving them. They keep digging and poking and picking at the wound even as it tries to heal. As a result, it remains raw and continues to bleed.

➤ You are not a victim. Others may have meant that you should be but it is imperative that you acknowledge to yourself and to whoever else will listen that you are not a victim, that your past however difficult, however painful does not and will not dictate your future. You are alive so the 'thing' failed to make you a victim.

➢ Not dealing with the past can destroy your future. It means you keep giving the past power to hurt. As you reduce visual contact with the past you see it less and reduce its impact on you. Looking at it continues to magnify it and to reel it continuously into the present.

➢ Don't keep title deeds to the issues you have dealt with. You don't need to refer to it as your problem: 'my migraine', 'my abuse', my pain'. As you continue to talk about it possessively you are giving it access to your inner circle, it won't go away and you won't get healed.

➢ A time needs to come when you have acknowledged what happened, you have sought help, you have forgiven yourself and the person/persons who hurt you and you have received God's healing. You then need to move forward and put that issue as far from you as possible, not because it didn't happen, but because you don't want it to keep affecting you and to mar your future.

➢ The painful 'thing' or 'incident' in singular or plural needs to be buried, it needs to be relegated to history which may be a painful one like slavery or like colonialism or abuse. It needs to be dealt with and buried and left in the cemetery not continually unearthed and brought home. It must be left in the place of and for the dead because it also is dead. Stop resurrecting it.

➢ The life you have is yours; God has given it to you. You can leave the reigns of it in the hands of your past and the people who hurt you or as you heal you can snatch those reigns back and begin to take responsibility for yourself, for your thoughts, for your actions and for your life. Set the boundaries you need around you so that you decide who and what is entertained in your life, who and what is allowed entry.

➢ You will not be healed until you decide that enough is enough and you need to move on with your life. No one can make that decision for you regardless of how much they love you. You need to get to the point where you are fed up of being angry, hurt, bitter, unforgiving and unforgiven. Only then will people come alongside you to help take away what you have been carrying on your own, only then will you be light enough to anticipate a bright future. You must move on.

Wrap it up

I read this on Facebook and thought it really appropriate and relevant, a précis of this whole book and a good place to wind down from.

> *Until you let go of all the toxic people in your life you will never be able to grow into your fullest potential. Let them go so you can grow. Robert Tew*

For us to really enjoy the future, to step into it with hope, we have to disengage and disentangle ourselves from people, habits, situations and things that have been binding us and holding us back. You can't run when you are embracing someone or if someone is holding tightly onto you. You need your arms to be swinging freely; you need your legs free to really kick off. So if there are things and people that are in your way, becoming obstacles, they need to be shifted. It's time to focus on your life and work out where you need to be and if those people have a different destination then you need to wave goodbye and move on. Like Abraham and Lot in Genesis 13, there are times you have to part ways even with people you love.

One of the things I really appreciate about life is that it doesn't have just one beginning. We are equipped with multiple entry points into the various aspects and facets of our lives. Whatever may have happened in the past does not have to be the final nail on a coffin containing you. Someone may have meant it to be but as long as there is breath in you, you can refuse to let that be the last note you sing. You can decide to encapsulate the last phase of your life and its challenges, throw away the keys, turn around and be the author of the next chapter of your life.

So regardless of what may have happened to you at some point in your life, if you are still alive there are changes you can make and there is a better future for you than what you thought you deserved because of your past. Your past can become powerless if you take the power from it, if you turn your back on it, if you bury it and refuse to exhume it when it is convenient to do so.

I pray that your community and your family is a safe place for children, and the vulnerable people that are entrusted to it. I pray that your children are safe in your embrace and that your family knows that you protect rather than destroy those entrusted into your care by God whether it's in your capacity as a parent, spouse, older brother, cousin, uncle, aunt or family friend. Don't be the one that destroys a life because of your anger, your misuse of substances, your perversion or whatever it is about you that makes you think that it is okay to inflict pain and cruelty on another.

May you be healed and may you be an instrument God will use to bring healing to others. Don't allow your story to end in tragedy. Determine to shame the pain of the past by becoming a conduit of healing for others. But above all, live the life God intends that you should, confer with him as you make plans so that your plans and his merge and you participate in and live the future he has already prepared for you. Snatch the reigns from your past and live a forgiven and forgiving life, you are not a victim, you are a victor.

Access denied

Hear the sound of fragmenting shells

as you rise above every issue

that has tried to destroy you

feel the crunch as you grind each piece to dust

with your own feet shattering the pain

with your own strength breaking the fetters

set your alarm lock the doors of your present

the past stealthily creeps to enter your future

but let it know speak to it 'access denied'

©farikanayi 28thFebruary 2013

Dear Reader,

Thank you for taking time to buy and read this book. My prayer and my desire is that it will make a difference in your life and in the lives of your loved ones. I want to encourage you never to give up, never to feel like you have to pack it in, never to despair. Regardless of how your life started the potential for it to improve and excel is always there. We have to choose to live and we have to choose to get up and keep going. There is always hope to the living. Hold on to it and seek help if you need it.

I would love to receive your comments after you have read this book. My website will contain more information on books I am working on and when I expect them to be published .I will also post events related to the books and publish event-related poetry from various poets. God bless you richly.

Fari

Author contact:

farikanayi@gmail.com

www.farikanayibooks.com

www.ingramcontent.com/pod-product-compliance
Lightning Source LLC
Chambersburg PA
CBHW072011040426
42447CB00009B/1583